Ne

Messie Kids

Books by Sandra Felton

Meditations for Messies
The Messie Motivator
Messie No More
Messies Superguide
The New Messies Manual
When You Live with a Messie

Neat Mom, Messie Kids

A Survival Guide

Sandra Felton

Fleming H. Revell
A Division of Baker Book House Co
Grand Rapids, Michigan 49516

Published by Fleming H. Revell
a division of Baker Book House Company
P.O. Box 6287, Grand Rapids, MI 49516-6287

Printed in the United States of America

Library of Congress Cataloging-in-Publication Data

Felton, Sandra.
    Neat mom, messie kids : a survival guide / Sandra Felton.
        p.   cm.
    Includes bibliographical references.
    ISBN 0-8007-5805-6 (pbk.)
    1. House cleaning. 2. Child rearing. I. Title.
TX324 .F4428 2002
648´.5—dc21
                                    2002001633

For current information about all releases from Baker Book House, visit our web site:

                http://www.bakerbooks.com

To those important people
with the most significant job in the world—moms

Contents

Acknowledgments

The more books I write, the more I become aware of all the people who are part of the process. This was never more true than with *Neat Mom, Messy Kids.*

Some of the people have helped me in personal ways. Ivan, my husband, offers support by his encouraging words and by doing more than his share so I can write. The moms in my family, my daughter-in-law Linda and my daughter, Lucy, contributed without knowing it by refreshing my mothering memories as I watched them mother my grandchildren. My personal and professional friendship with Marsha Sims, head of Sort-It-Out professional organizer service, has enriched my life across many years.

Many have helped with the writing process. By its nature, writing tends to be a solitary affair. However, contact with my critique group keeps my enthusiasm warm and my interest high. Rebecca White gave major help with the bibliography and other important detail work. Cliff Hanham's Latin research found *Quaerite ut abundetis* from 1 Corinthians 14:12 in the Vulgate. His finding adds a special and unique touch.

A book in progress needs friends for itself too. The editors at Revell do their jobs ably and enthusiastically. A special thanks goes to Bill Petersen, editor extraordinaire, for nursing this idea into acceptance. Lonnie DuPont Hull and Mary Wenger put it on track and kept it there. Mary Suggs did a wonderful job with editing. Sheila Ingram, gracious and helpful, was always there to answer questions and point me in the right direction. Many others do a yeoman's job, unrecognized by name but appreciated. Without those in the marketing, sales, distribution, publicity, and the like, this book would never rest in the hands or heart of a reader. I really appreciate all of you who work with Revell to move the book from the computer into the world.

The heart of this book is the experiences moms have shared as they follow their dream to create a nurturing and organized house. Together women have supported each other on the groups which meet online on the Messies Anonymous website, www.messies.com. Because of their contribution, this is not a book of theory. Their shared experiences make this book breathe. Thanks to you all.

A very special word goes to Karen Whiting. Although she contributed in many ways, one stands above all. Through her example I saw in action what I have tried to explain in this book. Early in her life she found her dream and has woven it through her family. Her legacy will flow for generations to come in her family and through her contributions in this book, to generations of other moms. May we learn to follow on that path.

How can I say thanks to God, who has brought me to this point and has enabled me through the years to contribute to others and be helped myself in the process? If we could see behind the tapestry of our lives, we undoubtedly would note his hand weaving what is good in our lives.

Like all of our brain children, this book is special to me. It was in this book Rosalie and I shared many life-changing insights that will change the lives of many moms and, through them, children who will in turn influence others. It has been fun and inspiring to write. Even so, as Huckleberry Finn concluded at the end of his story: "And so there ain't nothing more to write about, and I am rotten glad of it, because if I'd a knowed what a trouble it was to make a book I wouldn't a tackled it and ain't agoing to no more."

But I probably will.

Introduction
From Me to You

Let's Talk about the Kids

Somewhere in your life there is a someone who has a messy room, leaves the living areas cluttered, or does not help with the chores. Maybe all of the above. He may be a good kid in many ways, but this is not one of them. She may have wonderful qualities—in other areas. You fear for their future mates and you aren't satisfied with how it is working out for you on a day-to-day basis. You want the problem of their disorganized tendencies to stop for your sake and theirs.

Let's Talk about the Mom

You may be naturally neat and can't figure out why your kids didn't inherit some of this tendency. "What is it with these kids! Do they think I am a maid?"

On the other hand, you may be a not-so-neat mom who struggles with keeping order. You wonder how you can teach your kids when you aren't setting a good example and you don't have a handle on how to do the job yourself. The methods in this book will help both of these kinds of moms. You will need to become the coach of a family organizing team. You are the only one with the power and the interest to bring about the change you want. You are the only one reading this book, aren't you? I think that tells you something. More importantly, you have the dream of what your family and your home can become. Through you, changes will be made that will benefit your house, kids, and family.

Let's Talk about the Family

The goal of your family team is to create a house that nurtures and supports each member of the family. It is where everybody carries his or her share of the responsibility. Using the house as the playing field, the kids learn attitudes for living that will take them far beyond the house into adult living. Things like fairness, carrying their part of the load, planning ahead, caring about dignity in living space, time management, and all those other things that don't sound exciting but enable those who learn them to live a happy and exciting life.

Let's Talk about the Solution

The first part of the book focuses on you because you are the spark plug of change. The second part of the book focuses on the kids.

Step by step, using the ten powerful ideas found in the book, your family will begin to change and the house will follow. When you reach the end of the book, you will know what to do to create the home of order and dignity you want. That's a promise. You'll see.

You will also have discovered secrets that will carry over to making your family a wonderful dynamic unit in ways that flow way beyond the house. That's a promise too. You'll see.

An Orderly Home without Effort

ONE

Your Dream of an Ideal Home

It's a funny thing about life. If you refuse to accept anything but the best, you very often get it.

W. Somerset Maugham

You are probably reading this book because you are tired of working so hard to keep your house organized, neat, and visitor ready. You'd like to feel comfortable with the condition of your house, maybe even proud of it.

It wouldn't be so hard if it weren't for lack of cooperation from the family. Not only will they not do their part to clean it, they are actively messing it up! An active, modern, capable woman has better things to do than serve as a full-time, unpaid, frustrated maid. She has better things to contribute than pick-up work that could be done by any untrained worker. A loving mom needs a better relationship with her kids than yelling at them about clutter and not helping with chores.

Solving these problems is what this book is all about.

It's about the Kids

Let's get one thing straight. This book is not primarily about the house. It's about your kids and about how you manage them as they are growing up. You have a really big job in life—raising children to be successful adults.

There is one skill that will help them with everything they do. If you give them this skill, you will be giving them help for the rest of their lives. The skill is the ability to organize themselves, their living space, and their lives. What better way to teach them how to do that than as you interact with them daily in your home?

Do you want your children to have smooth marriage relationships? It will help if you teach them to be neat with their belongings. Do you want them to succeed in their jobs? Teach organizational skills. Do you want them to get out of the house on time tomorrow and in the days to come with matching socks, all of their papers, their keys, and peace of mind? Teach them how to do it now and it will become a natural habit serving them all the rest of their lives.

> A loving mom needs a better relationship with her kids than yelling at them about clutter and not helping with chores.

Let's get another thing straight from the beginning just to clear the air. This book is not about scrubbing and cleaning the house. Important as cleaning is, that's not the focus of this book. My goal is that you learn to create an environment where your family can grow, be refreshed, learn about life, and feel free to entertain friends. Such an environment involves how good your house looks, how well it works, and the interaction of the family members as they maintain it. In short, my goal is that you and your family begin to think of your home as the best place in the world for you to be.

What about Dads?

I guess this is where we should mention that, although this book is written to moms, dads are not excluded. Dads are very important in this whole process. Since that is true, some may wonder as they read this book why the fathers are not included more.

The facts of life are such that, although men are helping out more and more with the house and kids, the burden of solving the kinds of problems dealt with in this book generally falls on the mom. Hopefully, in your house, your husband does his part and supports you as you do your part.

Men, especially those in that growing group who are parenting alone, please feel free to read and apply any of the ideas here that you find helpful.

Getting It Right

As you read this book, you may be thinking of women around you who seem to be sailing through life, creating a satisfying and successful home, and training their kids with very little effort. These people do exist. They stand as testimony that it can be done.

They are getting it right, but getting it right doesn't mean that the house is perfect. It means that it consistently looks good and works well at the level they enjoy. And the family is working together, creating that environment.

These women know that getting it right means more than doing their housework well. They know there is something important about what they are doing, some higher goal, some unseen but vital purpose that "getting it right" in their housework serves. They also know that the only way to reach that something higher is to focus their attention on the mundane, boring, trivial, unimportant, and initially time-consuming aspects of the process (ugh!). They know that consistent attention to the little things is the secret of success.

Solomon wrote that parents are "the pride of their children" (Prov. 17:6). Kids love their folks pretty unconditionally, but which parents make their kids proud? Kids are proud of parents who, among many other things, can create a nurturing home. Whether kids feel it consciously or express it well, they are proud:

- when they sit down to a satisfying meal with their family
- when friends come over for a group get-together and it turns out "right"
- when they come home (maybe with a friend) to a supportive and welcoming home
- when they look around and consistently see beauty at home
- when they go to bed under clean sheets and a warm blanket
- when they get off to school in a good frame of mind with everything they need
- when they have created a room that expresses their personality and tastes
- when home is the place where they are most comfortable in body, mind, and spirit
- when the family works together to maintain order, dignity, and harmony in the home

Sometime, somewhere the thought will surface, "Wow! What a family! We did this!" And they are proud of their folks. That's worth working for.

The Soulful Home

The house is not just brick and mortar, rugs, furniture, and appliances. A real home, a soulful home, is more than a place where you can easily find what you need or where you can bring a friend without embarrassment. There is a comforting tenderness to a soulful home. Somehow, in the heart of hearts of the children, the cookies-and-milk thing translates into love. When the environment of the home is good, really good, the children, and other members of the family as well, think, *I am cherished,* and they breathe a deep sigh of contentment. Providing for the family's need for nurturing is no small accomplishment.

Frustrated Moms, Messie Kids

Let's get one final thing straight before we begin. This book is not just for moms who have their act together and whose houses would be perfect if it weren't for those pesky little Messies who live with them. It is not that simple.

Some of you may be struggling to keep your own life under control and wonder how you can possibly teach others to be organized. Not to worry. This book will give you a few supersignificant principles that will transform your life if you need to learn to be organized along with your family.

Neat moms can find help here too. Even superneat moms need to give thought to how they can best use their gift to teach their kids to organize. When you find organizing comes easy to you, it may be hard to know how to help those in your family who struggle with it.

Some superorganized moms may be so good at organizing that they don't need the kids at all. They prefer to work alone and let the kids concentrate on school-work and extracurricular activities. When the condition of the house is very important, it's easy to let that inappropriately become the main goal. Don't leave the kids out, even if it is easier to organize things by yourself. This book is for every mom who struggles with messy kids whatever her present situation. Both neat and disorganized moms need to learn how to relate to the kids and the house in light of their own organizing skills.

Often the mom who is working hard but is not getting the house under control would have a problem even if she lived alone. But the mess is definitely compounded by others. Now her work is on three fronts. She is struggling with herself, with the house, and with getting her family to do their part.

If you have the idea that I'm saying moms should stop being lazy and get in high gear creating a dream home, you are completely wrong. Women are already working hard, but much of the hard work is not accomplishing what is intended. The problem is that they are doing the wrong work.

What is the right work? That is what the rest of the book is all about. You must shift your focus and your ideas to make the changes you yearn for. If you do and put those new ideas into practice, you will have success beyond your wildest dreams.

We will concentrate on and apply these ten big ideas. They really are big, even if they look deceptively simple.

Idea 1: The house is not the problem. It's much more complex than that.

Idea 2: Working harder is not the answer.

Idea 3: Raising kids into adults who are able to function to their highest capacity is our goal.

Idea 4: The good Manager gains the cooperation of her family by involving them to the maximum of their ability.

Idea 5: Clarity about what you expect your child to do is essential to avoid confusion and conflict.

Idea 6: Consistency is paramount for success.

Idea 7: Strong bonding is the sled on which this whole program moves forward.

Idea 8: The Manager-mom holds the key to reaching her goals.

Idea 9: The Visionary-mom is the spark plug for this whole operation.

Idea 10: The house must be prepared to cooperate with your plans.

The process does not work by magic. It requires hard work and focus. But the results will be more than worth the effort.

Self-Inventory

But how will you do it? How will you get your family to do it? First, you need an idea that inspires. And then you need a clear understanding of how to create your dream.

Look around your house right now. What you see is a distinct reflection of yourself. I know others live there too and are a part of the problem, but you are the most powerful factor in what the house looks like. And you hold the key to changing it. For the house to change, you must change first. If you are not willing to make changes in yourself, your house and family will never achieve your dream.

At this point, you are probably satisfied if the kids keep their rooms neat and help with their chores without a lot of hassle. And you'd like to hop off the mean-mom and overworked-maid merry-go-round you feel like you are on most of the time.

> You are the most powerful factor in what the house looks like.

That's where we are heading. But you will find that if you do it right, other things will happen as well. As you strive to create the house you want and need for yourself and your family, you will learn things about yourself. The process will create positive changes in you and your family that could not happen in any other way. As you read this book, you will begin to see how you can make the changes that will affect your life forever.

Not in a Vacuum

This whole subject of creating a dream home does not exist in a vacuum. It's part of the larger realm of family living. Raising kids is a complex and multifaceted affair and includes playing, good conversations, really knowing your children and how they work, and caring about their individuality—wow! It's overpowering just thinking about all of the good things parents have to try to bring to the family.

Families can be lots of fun and very rewarding in many ways—most of the time anyway. We all have our moments when this is not so. The surprising good news is that the organizing plan you are about to undertake will strongly contribute to knitting your family even closer together.

If things aren't going well in your relationship with your kids, getting them to clean up their rooms and help with the chores can be an annoyance, if not an outright battle. On the other hand, when done well, involving the kids in housework can be the starting point for improving your relationship.

Meet Rosalie

Let's look at an example of one woman on the road to accomplishing her goal. We will meet her throughout the book and follow her progress.

Rosalie is a woman of character and quality. She has the dream of a beautiful home, a contented family. Her mother had always provided a gracious home. Rosalie took it for granted, because her mom had been able to achieve it without involving the kids. Rosalie just had never tuned in to how her mom did it. It had seemed so effortless for her, a natural skill.

Sure, Rosalie's mom had often worked hard. She would get cleaning urges and redecorate the house from time to time. Now and again she reevaluated and discarded out-of-date belongings. But there never seemed to be any struggle with day-to-day clutter. Soon after a meal, the kitchen was totally back in shape. Each morning, the bedroom was as presentable as it had been the day before. Closets and drawers stayed in good shape. Order was a given.

Now Rosalie was married. When she took that step, she never questioned that she would have a comfortable home. Mom had helped them set up housekeeping in a faraway city where Ben was in seminary studying to be a minister. When Mom returned home, she left two young people who had to figure out how to grow their own lives. Rosalie had a new career; Ben was laying the foundation for his; they made do and were happy. As in all dreams, the future looked rosy.

I met Rosalie when I was speaking at a women's meeting in Miami where we both live. At that time, she was nineteen years into her marriage. Ben was doing well in his career. Rosalie was working part-time four days a week. Her morning work hours let her be home when the four kids arrived from school. Then she shifted into high gear, chauffeuring the kids to practice, starting meals, doing laundry, supervising homework and baths for the young ones, and generally knocking herself out to keep on top of things.

She had approached me because she had finally had enough. I was not the first help she had sought. She had read books, actually had a library of them. She browsed the Internet. She showed me a posting she had found on the Internet in one of the forum groups she had joined in her search for change.

"Look," she said holding out the printed sheet at our first meeting. "This woman expresses pretty much my frustration. I have found out from other women on the Internet that I am not the only one. But I want to move beyond ending up like this before my children get any older."

I have tried lists and schedules and magazine articles and berating myself for being a slob and prayer and giving up.

I am surrounded by messes since my kids were quite young. My family doesn't cooperate in cleaning up because I don't set a good example. My kids are grown and messy. If I clean something up, it looks great, doesn't last more than a day. They have no respect for what is done.

The biggest and most fights are about who will do the dishes. We have distributed this responsibility in all ways possible. Now, since everyone has different work schedules, I am the only one who gets home at the same time each night, 5:30 P.M. It is "assumed" that I can make dinner and clean up the dishes. I say, no way. I will share, but not do it all.

I have been back to work for 3 years, full time. The kitchen is seldom clean, the dining room table is not used for eating, the living room has been freshly painted and has new furniture and now, laundry is dumped on the couch, but not folded unless I protest! No respect. The bathroom . . . you don't wanna know. I am disgusted with me and my family. What is wrong with us??? HELP. It's terrible to remember the childhood years of my kids as just conversations about chores and not getting them done.

Embarrassed

I understood completely. For the first twenty-three years of my married life I had used the same sporadic work-harder method and miserably failed. Before the kids came, the house was a mess. After they came, it was a shambles.

When the youngest was about thirteen, I woke up to the fact that if I took control of the house in some organized way, I could bring some order out of the confusion. I found an approach that showed promise of consistent improvement. By stressing out my brain and my body over a period of three months, using what was for me a revolutionary method I tell about in my book *The New Messies Manual*, I began to see change. Occasionally I asked my family to chip in or at least cooperate. But mainly, I was the kingpin, no, the only pin, in this operation. I did not have the strength of Superwoman. Only desperation to get out of this morass kept me going when I felt I could go no further. I was using the work-harder method and I was seeing some progress. It wasn't until later that I realized that there was much more to success than hard work.

Rosalie and I had a lot in common. As we talked I learned that Rosalie was a younger version of me. We decided to get together. I thought I could help her find a way out of her frustration.

"I'm exhausted," she said flatly as late afternoon sun poured into her living room window. This was the first of many hours we would spend together discussing Rosalie's goal for her home and how to work with her family to achieve it. Clothes needing to be folded were in a basket beside the hall entrance. A jacket draped over the chair and school books were piled on the dining room table, along with piles of bills. "I work myself to death and still it is not enough. I don't know what I'm doing wrong. Even if I had the time, I don't have the energy to do more.

"The kids are busy but they could help more than they do. And they could keep from making so many messes too. They are so careless. They leave things sitting around anywhere. We spend valuable time looking for shoes, baseball gloves, soccer shin guards, and who knows what else.

"I can spend an hour cleaning the bathroom and that night it's a mess. Sometimes it seems that there is no point to the whole thing.

"Ben, bless his heart, works hard. He gets home at seven after a long day. He often just drops his laptop on the coffee table in the living room. When he takes off his clothes, he lets them fall on the floor right next to the hamper. But he keeps telling me I should keep the house better," Rosalie sighed.

Beth, her seventeen year old, passed through the room on her way out. "Mom, Rachel and I are studying together over at her house tonight. Okay? I'll be home at nine. Test tomorrow. I'll get some dinner there. Thanks."

Rosalie nodded. And Beth was gone. She had been hoping Beth would pick up the twins from gymnastics. Oh, well, she would delay starting dinner and run down to pick them up. Or maybe pick up fast food—again.

TWO

The Three Homemakers in Your House

Take charge of your life. You are the only one who can—or should.

Every bride assumes that the life she is entering will be wonderful, beautiful, and satisfying. Love is the fuel that propels her into marriage. The last thing on her mind is housework. But there it is from the very first day and throughout the marriage.

Many wives and later-to-be moms bring a variety of good technical skills to their jobs in the house. But good skills are not enough. Women must be able to apply the right skills in the right way for their housekeeping to work. As life goes along, many hardworking women feel like the jockey in the following story.

There were two young hotshot farmers who competed with each other in every area of their lives. Both entered horses in the county fair race. Thinking to get the advantage, one hired a professional jockey. Sure enough, the two farmers' horses were far ahead of the pack in the appointed race, but as they were headed for the finish line, they bumped into each other and both fell, toppling their riders. The professional jockey jumped up, remounted, and won the race.

The owner who had hired him accosted him furiously. "What's the matter? I won, didn't I?" asked the jockey.

"Yeah," said the owner, "but on the wrong horse!"

Sometimes we are racing so fast, we fail to check whether we are on the right horse. Of course, we are working, but we need to make sure we are doing the right work. The following women, all of whom have many good skills, illustrate this point.

Good Skills

Marianne is great at crafts. She can make lots of cute arrangements and adornments for the home. But these things fall far short of making her home a lovely place to be. The craft materials are left out on the dining room table for days, the finished crafts can't be displayed because the tables are covered with other stuff, and decorations to be hung are waiting along the baseboard. What could have been a skill contributing to a beautiful home turns out to just make more mess.

Kara is an excellent cook. However, the mealtime schedule (if it can be called scheduled) is sporadic. Serving times vary widely. The main dish may be great but the salad, vegetables, and bread are added as an afterthought while the rest of the food gets cold. And the kitchen! Because of the lateness of the hour, dishes and pots are left to form crusts or soak or both. Kara often thinks ordering pizza is a better idea than cooking. She may be right.

Lucinda knows how to do laundry, dishes, and cleaning. Her skills are no problem. Why is it then that the house is often a wreck with dirty laundry on the floor, clean laundry unfolded in living room chairs, dishes unwashed, and the house uncleaned?

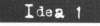

Idea 1

The house is not the problem. It's much more complex than that.

Lenore kept a neat house for the first few years she was married. When the first child came, she was able to keep up by working harder. But when more children arrived, all of Lenore's time and energy were spent on her family. Her abilities were stretched to their limits. More laundry, more cleaning, more cooking, more of everything overwhelmed her. She just couldn't keep up.

Having household skills is not enough to successfully care for a home and family. These capable women are ignoring aspects of homemaking that they must have to be successful.

The crux of the matter is this: The job of housekeeping is complex, and we must have three very basic, broad, and highly developed sets of skills working on all cylinders to accomplish the task, especially when children and husband are involved. We will call each of these sets of skills a personality.

Much of the confusion comes because we fail to notice that we must bring these three personalities into adulthood if we are going to be successful. These three personalities are the Visionary, the Manager, and the Worker.

- The *Visionary* walks down the wedding aisle, envisioning her first home with her new husband.
- The *Manager* translates the Visionary's dream into reality.

- The *Worker* sets to work getting it all done.

All three of these parts of our personalities are absolutely necessary for the house to become what each part yearns for.

The Visionary

Every really successful home starts with a dream. At the beginning it will be in embryonic form. Maybe, at first, the new bride follows Mom's style. Or maybe, as a statement of independence, she goes in exactly the opposite direction.

Eventually every successful homemaker finds a dream to guide her. Often this dream is so much a part of her psyche that she doesn't even realize she has it. But it's there, woven throughout her being.

And she had better make it a big one. Only a really great dream is worth working for. It will keep her going in tough times. It will give her strength when she grows weary. Without a dream, housework is just one job after another. With a great dream, each activity is part of a large and exciting whole.

The Dream Comes into Focus

Although women differ about the level of orderliness they want, every Visionary strives for a home that visually nurtures those who enter the home. Some require a high degree of order, clean surfaces, and an overall degree of neatness so that all doors can be happily left open. Others are more casual, hitting only the high points of housekeeping. But all have a vision, even those who seem never to have had a vision or to have lost the one they had when young.

In addition to wanting a house that looks good, all want a house that works well. They want a house where people can easily find their oft-used belongings, like keys and socks. Stored things are accessible and all family members know where they are. It is enjoyable to function in this house. The house works.

The true Visionary sees beyond the house. She wants, in the fullest sense of the word, that wonderful thing called a home. She envisions not only a wonderful environment but loving relationships of fun, intimacy, and fulfillment as she and her husband grow their family. As long as that vision is strong, the Visionary is committed to it in the deepest core of her being. She will work for it and resent anyone who interferes with it. But those interferences will come.

Cracks in the Vision

Sometimes the interference comes from within herself or her family. If she is the one interfering with her own dream, there are several things she may choose to do. She may hire outside help to come in and clean, seek therapy for herself, drive herself to work harder, or marry a person who is neat and may help her overcome her own tendencies. To overcome interference from her family, she may nag, scold, yell, set up schedules, beg, cry, flatter, or reason.

Sometimes the interference comes from messages sent out by society. Consider the message sent out in this *Chicago Tribune* article. Eileen describes her home with her eight- and ten-year-old daughters. "Our house is a minefield of Barbie shoes, odd crayons, game pieces and sheets of paper with one mark in the corner. Clothing is strewn from one end of the house to the other. Lost shoes are a daily fact of life in this house."

The article then continues, "What's wrong with all these kids? Well, actually, probably nothing." It then goes on to quote a psychologist who advises that, at this age, kids need to rebel, and parents should tolerate everything short of "having little crawling things on the floor."

Some people buy this approach and endure the unpleasantness of living in child-created clutter and chaos—at least for as long as they can.

But the Visionary cannot give up so easily. She does whatever she can because she cannot be content seeing the beautiful dream fade. Even after years of failure, when she thinks she is doomed to live without its fulfillment, somewhere the ember of the dream still burns. It won't let her rest until she achieves in reality that vision of so long ago.

Some people may call this dream having goals. But it is much more than that. Goals reside in the brain, the mind, the intellect. This dream has its home in the deepest part of the emotions, the will, the spirit. It is not cool and laid back. It is fixed and strong. If threatened, it becomes passionate.

The Manager

The Manager craves order. Pragmatic to a fault, this part of the personality thinks that all will be well if the correct system can be found and consistently implemented. The Manager buys books on organizing to locate the most useful organizational products and sets up systems for doing everything right.

The Manager may resent the Visionary who moves on to new areas, seeking beauty, harmony, and something better. The Manager appreciates the dream but she interprets it in terms of practicality: "If we can just get a good setup and stick to it forever, we'll be okay."

The Worker

Every woman knows the Worker part of herself very well. Nothing moves forward without someone to actually do the work. From the first day in her new home, the bride is busy making breakfast, clearing the table, washing dishes, cleaning, doing laundry, folding it, putting it away, making the bed, straightening things up, and the like. This may be in conjunction with her helpful husband and in addition to her work outside the home. The work is always there. When children come, she has more work to do.

The Worker part of the homemaker probably enjoys the activity of making a home as long as she is not overloaded by projects the Visionary imposes on her. She may be annoyed that the Manager wants to set up a system and make her a cog in that machine. She enjoys a personal sense of accomplishment, a feeling of power. She can accomplish much. She is capable. She lives in the present. She sees what needs doing and she does it.

The Place of Each Personality

We bring all three of these personalities to our first home and every one thereafter. Each has a crucial part to play in the success of what we accomplish. The Visionary looks into the future and forges ahead to accomplish great things. The Manager provides the plan to accomplish order. Drawing on the past and holding tight to that, she sets up the method for getting things done. The Worker has the advantage. Because she lives in the present and has her work immediately at hand, she sets about accomplishing what needs to be done.

If these three respected each other, cooperated, and supported each other, housekeeping would work without a hitch. But at many points, they work against each other. In the confusion, the Worker, who is closest to the immediate needs, takes over. Putting the Worker in charge starts out well but soon leads to disaster.

Rosalie's Response

Rosalie and I had decided to meet more or less regularly once a month or so. Her children had just returned to school from summer vacation, so we met at Rosalie's house. She had known I was coming and prepared ahead. We drank coffee at her kitchen table. Palm trees cast morning shadows through the French doors as I explained the three personalities to her.

She smiled wanly. Looking around her house, she said, "It doesn't feel like anybody is in charge here. I'm too tired to keep up with all that needs to be done. None of my personalities seems to be doing anything."

"But you started out as a Worker, didn't you, Rosalie? You thought that if you just worked hard enough and efficiently enough, you would succeed. But the housework snowballed. Each new activity, new child, new responsibility made you work harder and faster until you just couldn't keep up."

"What else could I have done? Somebody has got to do it. I ask my family to chip in when I need it. They help when they can. But they have very busy lives. It's just not working. I don't see how my friends, who seem to have their act together, do it. Do you see that house across the street? She's got more children than I do and yet her house always looks good. I'm over here working myself to death. She seems to be taking coffee breaks! What's going on?" she asked, sighing. "I wish I knew her secret."

"Let's step back and look at things," I said. "Can you see how the different parts of you vie with each other? One part is making new plans for the future while another is trying to keep things under control and still another is just doing the work at hand. There is no co-operation, no nurturing of each contributor, no balance. If you could wave a wand to change things, how would they be different?" I asked. "What would the Visionary in you dream?"

"I don't think I ever had a dream," she said. "I just thought things would happen naturally and turn out nice. That's what seems to happen to everybody else. They don't seem to be struggling like I am. And they are succeeding. I'm failing."

"But if you could wave a wand and make things different, how would they look?" I insisted.

Rosalie said she would like a house like the ones in magazines. She thought they were pretty, peaceful, and exciting. She could not put her finger on the style she liked but she would love for her house to be, as she described it, really, really beautiful.

She wanted her kids to keep their things neat, both in the house and in their rooms. Their rooms would look nice. Rosalie was on a roll and catching sight of a little bit of her vision.

She turned her attention to the kids and said she wanted them to better understand why she wanted the house to look nice. She wanted more help. "I'm not the maid they seem to think I am," she said with real fervor.

Then she spoke of her husband. "I love Ben. He helps when he can but he seems to think this is really just my job. I know he works hard but this is way too much for one person. We should be a team. He needs to back me up with the kids and help me with some of the work. I wish I had trained the children to help when they were little. It just seems so hopeless."

At first she had seemed to get excited. But now that she saw how far her dream was from the reality she was faced with day to day, she looked deflated. She realized that if she had ever had a dream, she had lost it. She was grieving the loss of that dream, of what might have been.

"For a minute you caught a glimpse of what could be for you. You may have said it in negative terms, but you knew it was there. Let me encourage you to go back to that dream with renewed hope. I want you to let the Visionary within you run free and imagine what a really successful house would be like in your life. What style would you like? How would you beautify your home? Imagine how your kids would act, what their rooms would look like. Think about what you would do with your free time if you didn't have to work all the time. Would you like to have friends in? Wonder and dream. That's where it all begins."

Rallying, Rosalie smiled a little and asked, "If I were to allow myself to dream, what could I do to make things totally different from the way they are now—if it's not too late?"

I knew she had opened the door a crack. I could see the light of hope shining out in one thin shaft. "There you go!" I said, not so loud as to scare her back into hopelessness. "To answer that question, let's see where you are in your housekeeping development. We all go through phases as we develop a successful household. After looking at where you are in the process, we can figure out how to move you on from there."

THREE

The Growth of the Ideal Home

If you have hope, if you have a dream, you make decisions in a different way.

When you started a home, you started a growing, evolving entity. Unfortunately most new brides or singles who set up their homes don't realize what they are setting in motion.

The main thing that they are thinking about is the freedom of being on their own. No more living in Mom's house according to her rules. Now the fledgling adult can do what she wants when she wants in the way that she wants. She is now the boss. The Worker within her reasons that as long as she does efficiently the work that needs to be done, she can indulge in the free-flying life she has dreamed of. Her concern is not what the household needs but what she wants. It is not long before this approach begins to cause trouble. She is in the infancy phase of developing a successful household.

If you understand the three phases of growth of a household, it is likely that down the line your household will be flourishing and you will be living a successful and fulfilling life. What's more, you will be satisfied that your family is growing in maturity, self-control, self-reliance, teamwork, and a sense of pride in the home you and they have created together. You will feel that you are on the road toward fulfilling the purpose for which you were created and put on the earth, a large part of which is to provide a nurturing environment in which your family can grow.

First Phase of Growth

When you first start, you, the Worker, are ecstatic. The sky is the limit. Hope for a better life drives you to put in long hours. You are optimistic. You derive energy from getting things done. Work is no problem because you are setting up your own life, building your own nest.

Things come up that you are not necessarily good at. You have not had much training in the running of a household. Bookkeeping, figuring taxes, cooking, all that laundry (who would guess there could be so much?), decorating, and cleaning are new experiences. No one job is extremely complex but each requires systems that you must develop and you may not know exactly how to set them up. A hundred other little things, like errands, getting things fixed, doctor appointments, and the like, begin to pile up. If you work outside the home, as many women do, you may find yourself panting as you run to get all of these things done.

Your husband, whose mom worked outside the home, is used to helping around the house. You're thankful that he pitches in and takes up some of the slack. Even so, you begin to fall behind, to drop some of the balls. The house begins to get a little ragged around the edges. The bed is left unmade. The laundry piles up. You eat out more or get takeout. Appointments are rescheduled or missed.

Then comes the blockbuster—a little one joins the family. Whatever was difficult before becomes impossible now. There are not enough hours in the day or energy in the body to carry on just by working harder.

Rosalie's Response

I had invited Rosalie to my house. She looked around curiously to see its condition. I like the stimulation of flowers, colors, and contrast in my decor. But she wasn't interested in decor. She was looking for evidence of organizational success. The house was neat and clean. What she could not see were the systems that were in place to bring a disorganized person like me, who had been forced to live an isolated life because of my clutter, to the place of being able to invite friends into my home. Rosalie would see those systems later.

As we talked, Rosalie admitted that she felt discouraged. She was beginning to face up to her situation. She felt hopeless. Overwhelmed. "I don't understand what has gone wrong. I work so hard. I want to give my children a good life. I take them everywhere they need to go. They have lots of classes they enjoy. I work hard to keep the house nice. I try to train them to do their part. You'd think they would be grateful for all I do and help out more. I love having a family. I would do anything to make it better for them and for me."

"That's the trouble, Rosalie. You are working too hard. You are already in the first stages of burnout. The only part of you taking care of your family is the Worker part of your personality. That's good, but you are ignoring the other necessary parts that must be developed if you are going to have a nice home and time for you to enjoy your own life as well.

"You have overdeveloped the Worker part of yourself and ignored the Manager and the Visionary parts. You have taken the easy way out. If all you want to do is accomplish tasks, you need to get a job as a housekeeper. Maybe at a hotel," I chided her as gently as I could.

"Listen, when you got married and had kids, you didn't know it but you signed up for a program that you were not prepared for. Few people are. Who teaches management and visionary goal setting to new brides? Nobody. But every mom who is going to be a success at managing her household has got to learn these skills.

To move out of the ditch you are in, you have got to change your outlook, your whole paradigm. You are going to have to abandon this Worker-only outlook, because it's not succeeding. And you will need to teach your family how to manage a house, to communicate, to work as a team. Your children are going to be growing up and living in their own homes someday. They will be ill-prepared unless you teach them.

> Kid power is the largest untapped source of energy in the world today.

"If you're willing, I'll help you," I said. "Can you shift from thinking that it is your responsibility to take care of the family and to understand that you are working toward the family meeting its own needs? You should be doing less and less. Eventually it will get to the point that if you are sick or out of town, the household will function just as well without you. Only then will you have a truly thriving and healthy family and, as a by-product, an orderly house. This can only happen if you encourage the Visionary and support the Manager parts of yourself."

Second Phase—Adolescence

When you give up the idea of being the kingpin of the home and doing everything yourself along with the occasional help from other family members, your home is on its way to adolescence.

When the Worker of the home wakes up to the fact that she can't do it alone and needs to be serious about getting help, she looks around for that help. What kind of help does she look for? Why more workers, of course. In the family, those are naturally her husband and kids. Kid power is the largest untapped source of energy in the world today. She has been trying unsuccessfully to tap into that power all along, but now she has a broader vision and she puts it into practice.

> **Idea 2**
>
> Working harder is not the answer.

Let's Divvy Up the Work

The Worker-mom's best prospect for help is her husband. She approaches him with her proposal. She needs him to take over more of the work of the house, let's say the bills, the yard—which he has been mostly doing anyway—and the garbage. She wants him to take ownership of those three areas so that she doesn't have to think about them anymore. He agrees and she moves on.

She divides up other jobs in an age-appropriate way among the kids and puts them on a chart, which she checks off as they do their jobs. First and foremost, they are each responsible for their rooms. She puts those things on the chart. Then she addresses the general tasks necessary for the whole house. They are mostly the grunge jobs that are generally uninspiring but necessary. She gives the kids a talk about fairness and working as a family. Then she sets up a reward and punishment chart for those who don't do the jobs assigned. Of course, she keeps those jobs that she feels are most in keeping with her talents and abilities, the cooking, driving, errands, and a myriad of others.

Feeling more relieved than she has for a long time, the mom sets about to oversee the jobs and check off the list. Those balls are somebody else's responsibility. "This is great!" she thinks. "Now I have time for the nicer things of life and the house will be nice too."

The Plan in Action

Things work well as the kids and husband begin their new program. The clothes are washed, bathroom cleaned, dishes cleared, and all in a timely manner. Mom marks off the chores on the chart, compliments the good jobs, gives the rewards, and where necessary, the punishments. Things are going pretty well. When there are slipups she attributes them to inexperience and old habits kicking in.

As time goes on, Mom begins to see parts of the system unraveling. Soccer games take Dad and the kids out of the house on Saturday afternoon when there is work to be done. Birthday parties lure the kids away at inopportune times. Homework cannot, should not, be neglected. Sometimes the children forget their jobs or are too tired to do them. And Mom feels like an ogre forcing extra work into their already busy schedules. Often granting amnesty, she feels the excuses are understandable.

So, just temporarily and on occasion, she waters the dog because his keeper is away, she takes the clothes from the dryer and piles them in the hall so she can get another load done, she picks up the towels and clothes in the bathroom at night when the kids are asleep, and she takes out the trash rather than live with it overflowing. In short, she is the Worker again, with just a little more help than before. And that's fading fast. The checkoff chart has become just another task for her to remember to do. The kids know their responsibilities and should be doing them automatically by now, she reasons. Though trying to be patient, she's getting tired of the moaning, groaning, and excuses. Soon the chart on the wall is still on Halloween, but the calendar is drawing close to Easter. The system has ground to a halt from its own weight.

Waking Up to Reality

The whole experience is a wake-up call. Somehow she doesn't have a family, she has a job—a hard, long, and pretty much thankless job. And it doesn't feel good. She hates it. *If they don't care, I don't care,* she reasons. And she lets things go. She no longer feels like she is creating a lovely home. She is just doing boring, mindless tasks. On some days she stays in her pajamas until just before the kids get home. She hopes nobody comes to the door until she gets some things picked up.

She orders out pizza a lot or throws something together for dinner at the last minute. The food pyramid becomes a rubble pile. Grape jelly is a fruit, catsup is a vegetable, and white bread is a grain. Sort of.

Rosalie's Response

"I have tried charts from time to time," said Rosalie. "They do work for a while but it is hard to keep them up. I just wish my family would look at it from my standpoint. The hardest part about this whole thing is feeling like people don't love me like they should or care about my needs."

I explained to Rosalie that the desire for fair treatment, for love, for caring from your family only goes so far. The mom who relies on that alone is destined for failure. To succeed, Rosalie needs skill, knowledge, and experience that she has not yet acquired. Mostly she needs a passion that will keep her on track and push her beyond her comfort zone into getting the skills she lacks in order to do the job.

Dealing with this problem is a real opportunity for personal growth. Really there is not much choice. The stakes are too high. The house and, even more important, the family depend on how well the mother learns and executes her job. To start a family and then fail to tend it is a terrible loss to everyone involved.

"Here's the bottom line, Rosalie," I said. "Your job from now on is to prepare yourself to do the job before you, growing a healthy family, one in which the house acts as a playing field for what you are accomplishing. When the family is working right, the house will work right."

Rosalie had given birth to four children. Now in some sense she was giving birth to something else very important. It would clarify a large part of her place in the world. It would affect the maturity of her children and the strength of her marriage. It was a family plan that would test and form her family in the most concrete way possible. She was building an entity that would be strong and function with or without her presence. In short, she was creating a mature family, not an adolescent family. Adolescents are strong but erratic. They are not known for wisdom.

Rosalie had a long life ahead of her. I tried to encourage her with the words of George Eliot who said, "It is never too late to be who you might have been." Even after they have left her house, seeing her grow and change would continue to influence her children.

How the Family Got in This Bind

Not all homes have to pass from infancy to adolescence to adulthood. Some homemakers start out knowing what they want and how to get there, never deviating far from their plan. For many of us it is not that way. What makes these successful homemakers different from those of us who struggle? Their outlook is completely different from ours. They do not focus on the condition of the house, the jobs, the chores, and so on. They focus on the goal they want to reach. Their concern is the development of the family members, including themselves, to their full potential both as individuals and as family members. The house is only a means to the end they want to achieve—a healthy, mature, functioning family. The beautiful, organized house then acts as a backdrop for the further maturing of the family members.

Idea 3

Raising kids into adults who are able to function to their highest capacity is our goal.

In recent years, however, several things have happened to make taking care of the house harder for women.

1. Houses have gotten larger. In 1953 the average residential space devoted to each American was 335 square feet. By 1997 it had swelled to 748 square feet. The median house size was about 1,100 square feet in 1953, but was 1,975 square feet in 1997. And house sizes continue to grow rapidly. In 2002, the average new American house is 2,250 square feet, double the 1953 size. That means a whole lot more house to clean and straighten.
2. We buy more products. According to Juliet B. Schor in *The Overworked American: The Unexpected Decline of Leisure* (New York: Basic Books,

1991), American women spend three or four times the amount of time shopping as western European women do. Of course, once we get our treasures home, we must care for them by storing them and cleaning them. Without noticing, women have traded leisure time for things.

3. We have adopted higher standards of cleanliness. Although we would expect products such as vacuums, washing machines, indoor plumbing, refrigerators, and stoves to have lowered the amount of time spent in maintaining the home, they have not. How we use our time has changed, but the amount expended has not changed.

One would expect the microwave to have made a significant change in the time we spend in meal preparation. Although the microwave cuts down on cooking time, it has not cut down on preparation time, which usually takes the most time when fixing a meal. Prepackaged products are quick to prepare, but the time saved is usually taken up with other activities.

Another example of this is laundry. With the invention of the washing machine in 1925, clothing that used to be worn for weeks unwashed could be changed once a week. By the '50s and '60s we were washing clothes after one wearing (or half a wearing.)

The habit has persisted and now we are automatically washing things that could be worn again without washing. Don Aslett says, "I don't want to shock you, but I believe in wearing work clothes a week, not a day" (*How to Do 1000 Things at Once* [Pocatello, Idaho: Marsh Creek Press, 1997], 96). Towels that could be hung and used for a week are tossed on the floor and scooped up to be washed on a daily basis. Outer clothing, such as pants or dresses, worn for a short time, are washed even though not soiled. It seems easier to throw clothes in the hamper than to hang them up.

Only one modern appliance has significantly changed how families use their time, and that appliance does not help with housework. It is the television. Close behind it and gaining fast is the computer. These two have gobbled up leisure time and put pressure on the amount of time families can devote to other things.

Another time factor is that many women have gone into the workforce. Obviously that significantly changes what they are able to do in their ever-growing house with its expanding demand for maintenance.

With the advent of modern household appliances and the two-car family, commercial services have diminished. Milk used to be delivered. Laundry was picked up, washed, folded, and returned to the house. Groceries were delivered by the local grocer. The doctor made house calls. Household workers used to be available and affordable. Now the parents, especially the mom, take up the slack in all these areas. Surveys show dads are beginning to take part in household chores more and more.

How Kids Fit In

The role of children seems to have changed significantly. I won't bore you with the history of childhood work, which involves changes from rural settings to the industrial revolution and on to the present. What is important to us in our time is that somehow in recent years, while Mom has been getting more and more stressed with all of the work she has to do, children have been doing less and less.

Parents want their children to have a good childhood, an idyllic childhood. To that end, they fill the kids' schedules with many fun and interesting activities. Parents seem to view childhood as a cruise and they are the cruise directors.

To some, it seems as though modern children have taken a place in the family similar to that of pets. They are enjoyed but are not expected to work as part of a family team. Housework takes a backseat to much more significant activities. Neither the parents nor the children seem to think it's important. It is just grunge work that takes up valuable time.

In many modern families, the job of children is to develop their potential in important areas of life during their childhood years. They are expected to be part of athletic teams, strive to do their best in schoolwork, develop artistic or musical abilities, go on extended trips to broaden their perspective, do community service, and generally work their little tails off improving themselves, all the while keeping an eye on self-esteem, of course.

After all this stress, they need to relax with entertainment such as movies, TV programs, and video games. And kids are kids. They need to have time to play and have fun.

When I read letters and talk to women who are frustrated and exhausted because the kids not only won't help but are consistently tearing up the place, it is clear that something has gone seriously amok. For their own sakes and the sake of the children, they need to make some serious changes. But how?

Third Phase—The Mature House

What Mom can do is shift her concentration from the house to the family. The condition of the house should not be the focus. The focus should be on how the family defines itself, what its common goals are, and how they work together to accomplish those goals. The house is the main playing field of these ideas.

Women who struggle unsuccessfully to keep an organized house usually do not have a clear vision of the family. Instead, they look at the work itself. That's because the Worker is in charge, moving herself and her helpers to get the house picked up so it will look good for that day. To solve this problem, the Visionary must take charge. She has a broader view, one that makes a meaningful whole of the little meaningless parts of daily life.

Comparing the Worker and the Visionary shows the important differences:

- The *Visionary* sees the meaning behind the work, the purpose of the organized and beautiful home. The dignity of the family, the rhythm of working together, the comfort of the whole are important to her.

  The *Worker* sees clothes to be folded, lunches to be made, animals to be fed, and bills to be paid.
- To the *Visionary,* each job completed leads toward the overall goal.

  To the *Worker,* each job completed leads to another job.
- The *Visionary* is future oriented. Keeping her goal for the future in mind, she decides what to do in the present.

  The *Worker* does what appears to need doing today and assumes the future will be pretty much like today.

Following the Visionary moves you toward your goal of a beautiful, organized home. Working together with your children, teaching them how to organize the house will not prepare them fully for life, but it sure will help with a big chunk of a really important part. "We should give conscious thought to the reasonable, orderly transfer of freedom and responsibility, so that we are preparing the child each year for the moment of full independence which must come" (Dr. James Dobson, *Dr. Dobson Answers Your Questions about Confident, Healthy Families* [Wheaton: Tyndale House, 1986], 55).

> **Idea 4**
>
> The good Manager gains the cooperation of her family by involving them to the maximum of their ability.

In the mature home the dynamics of working together as a team will help children grow into men and women who are capable of caring for themselves. They will be responsible adults and positive influences in the world. But this will not happen without careful thought and planning on the part of parents, especially Mom.

Rosalie's Response

Rosalie's house looked especially nice when I walked in that morning. I had no clue what method she used to get it that way. She seemed happy to invite me in.

As soon as we sat down, Rosalie began talking about some of her neighbors' homes that always seemed presentable. She wondered how those moms succeeded in getting the chores under control with the family as an integral part of the solution and not a part of the problem.

I listened sympathetically, knowing exactly how she felt. "Some neat houses may have controlling Managers who are driving themselves and their families crazy to keep the house pristine," I said. "The kids are under a yoke of constant tidiness. They may be learning to hate housekeeping, for all we know.

"Some houses may have Managers with a great deal of personal organizational skills and energy who do most of the work easily and only call on their families to chip in a little with maintenance. The Manager may be setting a good example, but she is not really training the children for life.

"And then, of course, some have Managers with great communication and organizational skills. They work well with their families to get the job done. The house is nice, the family is a team, and the mom is not frazzled. That style is what we are going for.

"There are other characteristics that make organizing easy for some people. They aren't sentimental so they can easily toss things out. You keep a lot more stuff than many women do because you are creative and can see possible uses for them. Other women are visually in tune so they notice quickly when things are out of place and it drives them crazy till they fix it. You are less in tune to visual pollution.

"They can stick with a job for a longer time than you are comfortable with. They remember things that need doing that may slip your mind. You tend to lose track of time but they are generally aware of it in some subconscious way. There are a lot of natural differences, not things that are good or bad, that make organizing come naturally to some and not to others.

"We've already talked about women's energy, Some can work full-time and not miss a beat when they get home. When you get home from your half day of work, you have to rest up to get your strength back. There is nothing wrong with any of these characteristics. They just need to be taken into consideration when you think about becoming the Manager of your house.

"Keep in mind that it's not for your sake or for the house that you are doing this, though both will be happier when you succeed. It is because you have created a wonderful entity called a family for whom God holds you responsible. For your family to fulfill its highest purpose, you, your husband, and your children will have to become the best you can be. You all will have to wake up to the possibilities before you as they relate to the family. Organizing the house is one of your best opportunities for learning how to do that.

"Let's think about some of the characteristics of a successful Manager you will need to make your dream come true."

Part 2

Put On Your Manager Hat

FOUR

Managing the Manager

The difference between "I can't" and "I can" is often "I will."

You may think that the heart of this book is the chapter about managing the kids. That is, after all, why you bought this book. But that is not the heart of the book. This chapter is the heart. When *you* learn how to function differently, the rest will follow naturally.

If your priority were just the house, you could legitimately use any means necessary to get it in the shape you want it. That would include yelling, threatening, going on strike to make your point, doing it all yourself, getting a cleaning service, or whatever else it takes to get the job done.

But the house is not your priority. Your priority is far more important than that. You have a dream to fulfill, a long-term goal of enjoying a harmonious home now and training your children so they can live really great lives as adults. You want them to fulfill the purpose for which God put them on the earth. That takes knowing a few important things.

Becoming a Successful Manager

There is a definite difference in the Manager-mom who is successful in reaching that lofty goal and the one who falls flat in the effort. It is often hard to pinpoint but it is necessary to try. The difference can be illustrated in this true story about David, a Texas guy who set out to train his new bird dog.

David read books and practiced, but try as he would, David couldn't get the dog to obey. So he went to a friend who had experience training bird dogs. After watching David try to put his dog through her paces, his friend said, "The problem is not with the dog. It's with the trainer. You're not giving her commands. You're just giving her suggestions. She's considering."

> **Idea 5**
>
> Clarity about what you expect your child to do is essential to avoid confusion and conflict.

Looking back on what he learned, David said, "I was confusing the dog. I was inconsistent. I was just uneducated about how to apply what I had learned from books. After talking to my friend I did three things differently. I made my directions to the dog much clearer. I was consistent in how I gave them. And I followed up to make sure they were followed. When I corrected those things, the dog got much better."

Obviously kids are not to be equated with dogs but we can learn something from this story. Like David, a mom who is getting little cooperation does not understand the difference between what she is doing and what the more successful Manager-mom is doing. On the surface, it seems to be the same. However, the successful one gets results repeatedly and over the long haul. The other mom gets spotty results, has to work hard at getting anything done, and finds that the room quickly falls back into chaos.

What are the differences?

Idea 6

Consistency
is paramount
for success.

The successful Manager has a burning dream and communicates it well. People resist change because they are afraid they will lose something. Your kids will resist the changes entailed in your plan for keeping the house clean, unless they see that it will pay off for them in the future. They will work toward a goal that means something to them. But their cooperation may not happen all at once.

Until they begin to buy into the plan with their hearts, you will have to hold fast to your vision, even when they don't see it. When you use your best managerial skills, down the line they will wake up to the idea that things have definitely changed for the better and are working great for the family—and for them!

The successful Manager has a strong bond with those she is managing. When you deal with the hard parts of working together, your bond with your child is strengthened. When you set up responsibilities, check to see that they are done, and assign consequences, you are building a history where you and your child learn about each other and how to relate. Your child will learn to respect your qualities and learn how to appropriate those qualities for himself.

Idea 7

Strong bonding
is the sled
on which this
whole program
moves forward.

During that time when you are trying to make a turnaround from the way things have been, your children need to be reassured that you really care about them. If you're home during the day, bake cookies or pies so the heartwarming aromas will welcome the kids home. Make a point to have a favorite snack waiting after school and share it across the kitchen table. That means a lot. If you work outside the home, make an effort to spend extra time with your child in the evening reading or watching a movie together. Chatting while sitting together sorting socks can keep the ties strong. When your children feel really cared for, they will be more willing to work with you toward a mutual goal.

The successful Manager is authoritative, not authoritarian. There are several different parenting styles:

- *Authoritarian.* Doesn't listen to the child and makes unilateral decisions.
- *Authoritative/Democratic.*

  Strongly structures the child's behavior and consistently monitors his actions.

  Relies heavily on a strong parent-child bond. Elicits the child's viewpoint and help in problem solving.

  Appropriately grants freedom when the child demonstrates responsibility.
- *Laissez-faire.* Listens to the child and grants unearned freedom.

The best approach, of course, is the authoritative/democratic approach. This can be illustrated in the way a successful Manager handles the issue of her children's rooms. I have interviewed many moms about their kids' rooms. I am struck by the differences I hear in what they tell me. Those who get cooperation consistently do things that are foreign to more tentative moms.

More than one in-control mom has told me that, when she has told the kids to clean up their rooms, the kids don't eat until the job is done. When I told this to one struggling mom, her helpless reply was that her kids would go into the kitchen and get food anyway. When I reported this to an authoritative mom, it was her turn to be shocked. "She has lost control of her kids!" she gasped. It seemed inconceivable to her.

More will be said later about the importance of supervising the child's behavior and developing a strong bond with the child.

The successful Manager is comfortable with being "boss." Successful Manager-moms don't believe that all family members are "created equal" as far as authority goes. They are not looking to have a pure democracy where everybody has a vote, because they know parents alone bear the responsibility to grow a wonderful family.

Robert Wolgemuth, the author of *She Calls Me Daddy* (with Gary Smalley, Colorado Springs: Focus on the Family, 1999) and his two grown daughters, Julie and Missy, were interviewed by Dr. James Dobson on the *Focus on the Family* radio program. Two questions were part of their growing up. When necessary, the dad would ask, "Who's the boss?" On the program, the girls demonstrated how it worked in childhood when they answered in unison without hesitation, "You are." And when he asked, "When do you obey?" they answered quickly, "The first time." Obviously he wore his "boss" hat comfortably. It was clear from the interview that he had raised two lovely and happy girls into womanhood. It was just as clear that they had a strong bond with the "boss."

The successful Manager is logical and nonemotional about problem solving. Authoritative folks never cease to amaze me in how calmly and decisively they respond to troublesome situations. Jane quietly reminded her daughter that if she didn't keep her clothes off the floor and take care of them, she would put them in a trash bag and take them to a local charity. She took the same approach with toys.

It wasn't a threat, just information. Her view was that if her daughter didn't value her clothes enough to take care of them, she should not have them. This approach was a part of her lifelong belief that children should be responsible for how they live. Since the daughter knew the mom's values clearly and since mom had followed through once or twice, the clothes were picked up without rancor.

The successful Manager is tough but not mean. Children will sometimes think that Mom is being mean because she requires more from the child than the child is comfortable giving. Nobody likes to be considered mean. Real meanness has no place in an adult's dealings with children. But a good mom will be called on to be tough.

When kids recast appropriate toughness as meanness and say Mom is "mean," they are testing the parent's authority. By this accusation, they are also diverting blame from whatever they did wrong onto Mom's "meanness." When this happens, reply happily, "Great! You are beginning to get the picture. I am very mean when I have to be. Remember that the next time this situation comes up."

When you score your points with something of a twinkle in your eye, they know you know what just transpired in this game—and you won. In some ways this is reassuring to the child because every child wants his leader to be strong enough to manage both the child and the forces of the outside world. You gain respect when you hang tough.

But there is a more important issue here. You and I know what the children don't know. If we wanted to be really mean, we would let them grow up irresponsibly. But because we care, we have to work with their behavior and train them to live productive and enjoyable adult lives even when they don't want us to.

There is a time to be tough but there is a time to touch those softer parts of your family in a comforting and kind way. You need to open your heart and your mind to them and be vulnerable. Without that approach, toughness just looks like meanness to those you are leading. If you combine kindness with leadership, you can lead your family into the fray of the worst disorganizational problems and come forth victors.

> If you combine kindness with leadership, you can lead your family into the fray of the worst disorganizational problems and come forth victors.

The successful Manager knows her kids and is willing to work with them in the way they respond best. When I was teaching, parents would often come to me about their children who were getting into trouble in school. I was struck with how often the parents and kids seemed to be mismatched. Sweet, kind parents were overpowered by the tough, strong-willed kids we were discussing. Some of that may be happening in your house. Naturally low-key, kind parents need to rev up to meet the needs of their more difficult kids, even when it doesn't come naturally.

Often kids with powerful personalities grow up to be real leaders in adulthood, but they need the right kind of handling when they are kids to give them what they need and for the family to survive their presence. Obviously, naturally sweet and compliant children don't need the strong direction that resistant children do.

Whatever the personalities of your children, you need to evaluate and find what works for them and be willing to make adjustments in yourself to meet that special need. Children are hungry to be known, really known. When you take the time to get to know them and adapt to their particular needs, that is the highest form of caring.

The successful Manager is fair. When a Manager begins to use her rightful authority, she must be careful that she does not abuse it. There is an unwritten, unconscious contract between parents and children. Each holds certain expectations of the other based on fairness.

One of these contract expectations is that parents will not require too much too early of their children. Children understand that under some circumstances they must carry a heavier part of the load than they would ordinarily. They don't mind the work when it makes sense to them that they do it. But they do mind having to step inappropriately into the responsibility of an adult. When an adult, because of stress, misguided judgment, or any other reason, abandons appropriate responsibility and piles domestic burdens on the available child, resentment brews because the contract of fairness has been broken.

Another one of the contract expectations of children is that the adult will prepare them to achieve in adult life. They may not say it. They may not really be aware of it. They may resist the training. But when adults fail to prepare them for adulthood, on some level the children understand and resent this as well. You have an unwritten covenant with your children to prepare them with the skills and the mental approach necessary to do their adult jobs.

The successful Manager teaches clearly. What we are teaching is not brain surgery. It is not deep philosophy or heavy theology. Don't make the mistakes some of the others of us have made by trying to do some fancy-footwork teaching.

I recall deciding I would teach my youngest son that spiders are arachnids, not insects, by using intuitive teaching. At this time Spider Man was a popular TV cartoon character. I decided to sing his theme song, "Spider Man," using the words, "Arachnid Man," instead, which I did faithfully. I was confident my son would have one of those aha! experiences, putting two and two together and realizing that spiders are in the arachnid family. Later he told me that he was almost an adult before he realized why I was singing the song wrong. Intuitive learning definitely has its limitations. Teach simply and clearly.

> You have an unwritten covenant with your children to prepare them with the skills and the mental approach necessary to do their adult jobs.

Adrianna was committed to the "example only" approach. Tired and angry, she complained that her husband and teenage sons kept throwing their things around for her to take care of. She kept doing it because she was confident that her consistent example of service and orderliness would some day click in and they would naturally begin serving others and helping around the house.

She was teaching them, all right. She was teaching them to shirk their responsibilities and instead take advantage of someone else. At this point, you are probably wondering, like me, what those boys' dear wives will be dealing with when they leave their servant mom.

For our purposes, Isaiah's advice to teach "precept upon precept; line upon line, . . . here a little, and there a little" (Isa. 28:10 KJV) probably applies best. Moses tells his followers to teach their children diligently by talking to them in various settings (indoors, outdoors, walking, sitting, getting up, going to bed, and so on) and by writing down the important things and putting them in visually prominent places (Deut. 6:6–9).

The successful Manager takes training and support for the children seriously. Sure, it is easier to do it yourself without hassling the child or to take the heavy-handed approach and send the child to his room to clean it alone, threatening punishment if he doesn't do it immediately. Both of those are tempting but they do not meet the child's needs.

The successful Manager understands that:

1. Skills must be taught carefully. First show how to do it. Then, do the job with the child several times. Finally, give the full responsibility of the task to the child *and* stand by for inspection. Check from time to time to see that things don't slip.
2. Some kids lack organizational aptitude and need more training than others. Break the task down to simpler parts. Draw or take pictures or write out steps as reminders. Post them in a prominent place.
3. Working alone is hard. Work together with the child or get him a partner even when the child knows what to do and how to do it. Working with a friend is fun. Sometimes it works well to have siblings working together. Sometimes not! Use good judgment on that one.

The successful Manager makes it fun. Games and other imaginative activities make cleaning up fun, especially for the little ones. Your innovations will signal that changes have taken place in the house and things are (not will be) different. Some ideas you may try are:

- Set the kitchen timer for more time than it should take to do the job. Tell the children that if the room is clean before the timer dings you will use the left-over time to get ice cream and read them a story or play a game.
- Have an unusual inspection. Can Mom lie down on the floor and wave her arms and legs without hitting anything? Can Dad stomp around on the floor, dinosaur style, and not crush any toys?
- Put on a peppy tape or CD and work to that.
- Divvy up the toys into a container for each child. See who can get them into the right place first. This assumes that you have a "right place" prepared. Make sure the younger ones get fewer toys to put away.
- Make a categorizing game out of it. "Pick up everything soft." "Put away everything that has green on it." "Let's put all of Benny's toys in this box." Playing a march during this time will happily move things forward.
- Give your child a special apron, feather duster, and maybe even the especially designed family T-shirt that will make cleaning up feel special.

> Delegating is not asking for help. It is the heart of managerial excellence.

The successful Manager knows the importance of delegating. Some moms can't get over this hump. They feel uncomfortable asking for help. Delegating is not asking for help. It is the heart of managerial excellence. It is the coach setting out his game plan and sending his players out to execute it. Without delegating, you will not reach your goals for your home or your family.

Most adults don't realize the multiplicity of jobs that they have taken on little by little that only they can do: banking, bookkeeping, price comparisons, comparative shopping for household needs, straightening out insurance problems, meeting with financial advisors, transporting kids to events, filling out applications, and a host of other responsibilities they cannot delegate. This makes it imperative that they delegate the basic household jobs the kids can and need to do.

Trying to do it all yourself or delegating in a haphazard way on an as-needed basis cuts the heart out of any successful managerial program.

The successful Manager operates by agreements.

Family meetings are an essential part of the Manager-mom's plan. It is at these meetings that you let everyone know that things will be run differently, with the load of family work shifting from your shoulders to the shoulders of the family team.

Don't dump the whole load unceremoniously at once. Avoid the "I'm sick of being the unappreciated servant" speech. Start with just a few changes. Pick out several hot spots that are causing problems for you on a regular basis. Maybe it is the morning routine. Perhaps it is the condition of the kids' bedrooms or the mess in the bathroom after baths or the result of the poor aim at the toilet bowl.

Explain your goal clearly and ask if there are any suggestions on how to solve the problem. You may be surprised at what the family knows that you have overlooked. Bill may say, "Jerry leaves his toys in my room. It's not fair that I have to pick his stuff up and take it to his room."

Clearing away a lot of little hitches and resentments can go a long way toward getting your organizing show on the road. But this is not your goal. Your goal is to develop a consistent and orderly plan for the house for which everybody takes ownership.

Once you have introduced the subject of the hot spots and let it sink in for a few days, start with three routines, morning, after school, and evening. Write down the bare bones of the plan with the family's input. Don't overdo; list only the main things to start with. Too much change will overwhelm the troops. Remember also, you are going to have to supervise these behaviors, so you don't want to get more started than you can easily supervise.

List each person's part in the plan and post that on the wall in his or her room. For example, to start with, let's consider just the morning plan for Jamie, who is eight.

- Get up (set a certain time)
- Make bed (take a picture of his bed, well made, and put it on the wall)
- Get dressed (with clothes picked out the night before)
- Eat breakfast (whatever is your family custom)
- Put dishes in dishwasher (you must make sure it has been emptied)
- Brush teeth and wash face (you set the standards here)

Many of these things he has been doing more or less consistently, but things like the bed and the dishes in the dishwasher may be new.

Now comes the backbone of the management program—consequences for not complying. And trust me, children will make it a point not to comply because they need to test to see if you are really serious. They don't believe your words until they see your actions.

> They don't believe your words until they see your actions.

Set up consequences with them that are reasonably easy to apply. You make suggestions if they don't have a good one. Ask them what they would do if they were you and their child did not do his job. You may get some good ideas from the children, but you have the final word.

The consequence for dishes not put immediately into the dishwasher may be that you will put them into the dishpan so he can wash them by hand as soon as he gets home from school. When consequences are more difficult than the job itself, the child soon learns to do the job.

The consequence for not making the bed may be that you make it and he has to pay you from his allowance. If he leaves toys out, they may have to go to jail for a few days as punishment for being in the wrong place. They were sort of jaywalking. You choose the consequence that works best for you.

As long as the consequence fits the misdeed, your children will feel that the plan is fair. Fairness is very, very important to humans, especially children. When they test to see if you are serious and you carry out the consequence, you only need to remind them that this was what they agreed to. Write the consequences in a notebook so nobody will have any question about what was agreed.

Have family meetings once a week or so. This helps the family stay involved and interested in the plan. By having these family meetings, negotiating ideas and plans, listening respectfully to others, and planning for the good of the family, children are being trained for adulthood in ways that cannot be underestimated. This training will contribute significantly to their success with their families and jobs.

Wow! What a mom you are! What great adults they are going to be!

Rosalie's Response

Rosalie and I met for coffee at a sidewalk café on a Saturday morning. As we sat under the pebbled shade of a tamarind tree, she slabbed butter on her muffin as she drank her coffee. How did she stay so slim? I had ordered coffee but turned down the pastries.

"I've had a real revelation this week," she began. "I'm beginning to realize I have not been managing at all. I didn't even know I was supposed to be looking at my family as a team. I've been trying to manage my family without a training manual to tell me what to do or how to do it."

"It's true," I said. "Most women have had a sink-or-swim alternative. They either did it naturally or they sank. Most have been keeping their heads above water to some extent by working harder. Some manage pretty well until they finally reach a point beyond their managerial skills. But many women sink when it comes to management. They didn't know how to switch over from the work-hard approach to the management approach. It's a common problem."

"I came across a couple of posts on an Internet group for moms. Look at these. The first one points out my feelings about the work I do. The second pinpoints the need my children have, whether they know it or not, to be included in housework," she said, handing me the printouts.

I read while she sipped her coffee and watched the cars go by.

The first one read:

One of the main problems I have is delegating. I am horrible at this. I saw a cartoon today where the brother had agreed to be the sister's "slave" for a week (so she wouldn't tell Mom on him!), and the things he was doing for her reminded me so much of how I seem to "wait" on my children.

The second said:

You know, when I was a kid, I always wanted to help out my mom regularly, but any time I suggested that something be my job, she would just go ahead and do it herself. When I asked her about it, she said, oh, she had just gone and done it before it occurred to her that I was willing. She just went ahead and did just about everything for us, meaning no harm, but I think that attitude was really detrimental in a few different ways!

I think that we all need to know we can contribute and are important to our homes and our world, no matter how young or old we are.

When I looked up, Rosalie continued, "You've gotten through to me with the idea that I should switch over to managing, but now I'm stuck with the problem of how to begin. If I just jump in there with both feet, I'm afraid I won't know what to do and my family will revolt.

Idea 8

The Manager-mom holds the key to reaching her goals.

"When you said that we needed to operate by agreements, I realized this thing was for real and would mean I would have to change—and my family too. This is going to be a big change. They are used to the way things have been all along and so am I. You know, if they could just be a little more cooperative, we could avoid all of this about family meetings and lists. To make it work, I will have to change, supervise, and give consequences. I'm not sure I'm up to this whole thing."

"This is not the time to decide if you are up to this," I laughed. "The question is not whether you are going to do the job. It is whether you are going to do the job well.

"It is hard to change habits. It will feel uncomfortable for you and them. It is only natural that they will want to return to what is familiar. But it is worth it to stick to your plan until it feels familiar and your plan begins to pay off for everybody.

"In the end, once you get a pattern set up and your family has settled into the new scheme, you will have less work. But you will find that the issue is not how much work you are doing; it's whether you like the work you are doing and think it's worthwhile.

"I can tell you that picking up things and yelling at the kids to do their part is not fulfilling. It's just a draining job. Successfully managing a family and developing children into responsible and productive adults is exciting and exhilarating, definitely worth doing!"

I explained to Rosalie that she needed to think about how she was going to measure her progress. She needed to think in terms of time intervals. Where did she plan to be in three months, six months, a year, two years? How would she know if she was hitting those marks as she went along?

"Listen, any plan is better than no plan at all. You need a written plan for yourself and your family so that the members of your family know what is happening and where they fit into it. If you fail to write it down, you show that you are just playing around with one of the most important things you will ever do in your life."

Idea 9

The Visionary-mom is the spark plug for this whole operation.

I took a sip of coffee to let that sink in. "Right now you are looking at your own limitations. Are you going to allow your personal limitations to squash what this family could become? Letting your kids go out into the world without the best you could give them would be enormously disappointing. Seeing them struggle as adults because you failed to teach them would make you very sad and probably guilty.

"You can do it! Keep your vision alive and begin to shape the present against what you dream for your family. All of these ideas and plans will begin to take their place as a part of achieving your dream. You will begin to look on the family meeting and any other ideas you adopt as allies in the wonderful work you as a Manager-mom are doing. Your family can't help but pick up on your attitude."

Rosalie spoke with a certain confidence in her voice as she recounted that she and Ben had been able to have only one child, Becky, although they had wanted a larger family. Then, lo and behold, five years later Rosalie gave birth to the twins, and eight years later little Jo surprised them. They were delighted, even though having their children so far apart would spread her mothering over a lot of years.

Rosalie thought that she and Ben had done a lot of things right. Her kids are all really good kids. But for the first time she saw she had a key position in the managing of the whole scheme. For the first time she saw she was not just a member of the family who happens to be the one who cares about the house. She was not the one who was fully responsible for doing all the work in the house either.

Here she stopped, threw back her shoulders, pointed at her chest, and said triumphantly, "I have a special place in the family because, I am the Manager! I think I'll get a button made that says MANAGER just to keep that thought in my mind. And to let the family know my job.

"Well," she hesitated, poking her fingers at muffin crumbs on her plate, "I don't know if I really will have a button made but I'll tell you this. For the first time in my married life, I see what I am supposed to be doing in this area of the family. I've got Manager written in my heart."

"Now that you have caught the excitement of what is before you," I said, "let's look at some issues you may encounter when you begin to move forward."

FIVE

The Manager's Changing Attitudes

To be what we are, and to become what we are capable of becoming, is the only end of life.

Robert Louis Stevenson

The Manager decides to do her job. Fired with desire and an ever-increasing knowledge of what to do, she steps up to the managerial plate. But when the ball of everyday decisions starts coming her way, she finds that some of her own strongly held attitudes keep her from moving forward.

These attitudes are sneaky. Many masquerade as helpful outlooks that will enable us to be really great parents. Let's examine these attitudes a little closer and look behind a few attitude masks to see if they fulfill their promise.

Some parents don't want to use the little time they have with their children dealing with keeping the house neat. Parents who arrive home at six, seven, or later in the evening on weekdays have very little time with the children. Weekends are the only time for fun. A dad told me that he and his wife don't bother their preschooler about picking up her toys and other things because they want to enjoy her in those short hours. Who wants to waste time together by grousing about rooms, chores, and the like? These parents feel they are keeping their priorities straight.

It is true that bonding is more important than housework. But the two are not mutually exclusive. When parents avoid discussing responsibilities with their children, because they are afraid it will interfere with bonding, the kids miss out on a really important part of their growing up years—learning how to be contributing members of the family team.

Some moms are committed to creativity and fun (translate that messes) for developmental reasons. These moms feel that the experimental, free-flowing approach to learning is very important. I was one of the moms who let my children use the house as a giant laboratory in which to experiment. I assumed the children were developing gross and fine motor skills, visual awareness, creativity, and many other abilities. I hesitated to limit the number of toys or to restrict the areas of the house where they could be used. I was flexible with time limits as well. I had very few boundaries.

Although moms like me are frustrated and frazzled when their parenting style leads to chaos, their commitment to what they perceive as good mothering stymies any change that would involve limiting the children. They are willing to put up with the mess for the sake of what they consider good child development.

But way back in the recesses of reason, there is a nagging voice whispering that something about this is not quite right. There is another kind of development that is being neglected. As a general rule, to develop efficiency and organizing skills, children benefit from the most structured environment that the mom and child are comfortable with. Avoid the creative laboratory approach that doesn't require responsibility on the child's part.

Some moms want to be heroes. First, let's consider the real-life story of an office worker in a doctor's office who was constantly being interrupted by other staff people to locate something they needed. As a patient waiting in an examining room to see the doctor, I suggested a system that would make it possible for everyone to know where things were without bothering her. Closing the door and lowering her voice, the office worker said, "I don't want them to be able to do it themselves. This is my job security."

Some moms have the same attitude. Not that they are likely to be fired! They are, however, afraid their children will love them less if they require them to do anything.

Some moms think that "housework" is a waste of the child's time. Everybody knows that childhood is the optimum time for learning. Children go to school, of course. Then they take lessons, like piano, gymnastics, and ballet. They play sports and participate in clubs. Somewhere along the way they fit in homework and relax by playing and watching television.

When moms view this kind of learning as most important, they place living skills, family teamwork, and household responsibilities way down the priority line. These moms hope that when the child reaches adulthood, the skills needed for responsible adult living will automatically kick in. For now, they are training their children in other skills.

There are some experts who suggest that disorganized children don't necessarily turn into disorganized adults and that parents should "cool it" somewhat concerning training children to be organized. Sometimes the children develop as the experts predict. Often they don't. My observation is that many untaught kids are left to struggle without the basic organizational skills necessary to pull their own weight in life.

Some moms find it easier to do it themselves than to teach it. Rachel feels that she struggles unnecessarily with living successfully today because she wasn't taught how to take care of her family. Either her mom would hassle her about cleaning up her "slobby" room until she cleaned it or, she says, "Most of the time she would just clean it up herself to her own satisfaction. Now it's like I almost expect the house to just be clean because it always was and I never had to do it. I also never learned to cook, not even to brown hamburger meat or to tell when food or milk was spoiled, because she is an excellent cook, but never wanted, nor needed my help."

Some moms overreact if they were overworked as children. The Manager-mom who was overworked as a child will hesitate to ask her children to help her around the house. "I'm not going to do to my children what my mom did to me," says the grown-up who goes to the other extreme with her children. Her judgment is clouded by her unfortunate background. As a result, she continues to be overworked as an adult—and her children don't learn valuable lessons.

Some moms think that if they let their children rebel by not doing their jobs, they won't rebel in more dangerous ways. An article in the *Chicago Tribune* by William Hageman (Jan. 30, 2000) investigated parental attitudes about organizing. A mom and her fifteen-year-old daughter laughingly describe a disaster area with food and dirty dishes rotting in the rooms ("it dries like a piece of art"), things stuck to the floor under the beds ("so it never moves"), and things flung around ("Yes, but I know where I threw it"). Another mother tells how her two daughters, ten and eight, "have strewn things from one end of the house to the other." Losing things "is a daily fact of life."

In that same article, a psychologist, Amy Beth Taubleib, author of *A to Z Handbook of Child and Adolescent Issues* (Boston: Allyn and Bacon, 1999), advises that this is usually just normal rebellion and "children need to rebel." Rebelling by being messy, she advises, is "so much better than 12 pierce holes or going out and stealing." When put this way, having a kid with a messy room can look like a positively desirable situation.

Parents often echo this kind of thinking. Those who allow their children to be very messy often state that it is not very important whether kids learn to be neat or not. They have various ways of thinking about this.

- The kids will get neat when they have homes of their own.
- Children have the right to keep their rooms however they want. It's a privacy issue.
- We don't want to nag and yell about cleaning the room or chores. We pick our battles.
- I'm just grateful that they aren't doing drugs or becoming criminals. The mess is too small a problem to worry about.

There is some truth in all of these statements, but they overlook some very important factors in the child's life. Swallowing these ideas hook, line, and sinker serves to get the parent off the hook of having to be responsible for this important area of training for their children.

Expressing Your New Attitudes

Once you have challenged your erroneous attitudes, it is time to change your behavior. The first behavior to change is how you communicate with your child. Previously you dared only hope she would listen. As the Manager-mom, you speak with the expectation she will not only listen but respond positively to what you say. Many parents use the following four well-known communication steps very successfully.

You may feel awkward using these prescribed steps. You may learn to appreciate them, however, when you see how much better this simple approach works than nagging or talking till you are blue in the face without results. Or you may find a way that works better for you with your child. However you do it, communicate clearly with your child, so she will understand your expectations.

First, you deliberately approach the child and stay close to her, with your attention focused on the conversation. Yelling across the room as she goes by won't work. Then you use these four steps, which are probably familiar to you and your older children already:

- State your view as an "I" message. You simply state how you feel. "I feel frustrated when you . . ."
- State your desire. "I want you to . . ."

- Ask for a commitment. "Can you commit to that?" Or for younger children, "Do you think you can do that?" They should respond in some kind of positive way.
- State a consequence. "Good, I'm glad to hear that, because if it doesn't happen that way . . ." (and you state the consequences)

Here is an example of how that conversation might go in a specific situation.

"I" message: "You know, Bill, when you drop your clothes on the floor beside the hamper instead of putting them in the right section of the hamper, I feel like you don't care about what's important to me. Not putting your dirty clothes in the hamper makes doing the laundry harder for me."

What you want: "What I want is for you to put your clothes into the hamper just as soon as you take them off."

Call for a commitment: "Can you commit to doing that?"

Then Bill may reply, "Okay, I'll try." You know and I know that saying "try" is just a way of deflecting responsibility for action, but you can accept it at this point

Statement of consequence: "Great! That means a lot to me. You need to know that if I do see any clothes on the floor, I'm going to put those clothes in a box for you to wash. I wash only what is in the proper section of the hamper."

Of course, Bill may try to divert you by saying, "You sure are getting picky lately. You didn't used to be that way."

Don't fall for that diversion. Undeterred, you stick to the point. "That may be, but you need to know that if you don't . . ." and so on.

Prepare for Challenges

You should expect testing of your resolve, genuine forgetting, and a multitude of other things that will challenge this simple plan. Since children are children and new habits are hard for any of us to form, don't be surprised if you need to remind and encourage them. It helps to work beside them, offering assistance with big jobs. This will go on for years. Just because they know how to do the job and fully understand that they should do it does not mean that they have the attention span or the maturity to do the job without your involvement.

In a 1989 study, Elizabeth Crary (Elizabeth Crary, *Pick Up Your Socks . . . and Other Skills Growing Children Need*, [Seattle, Parenting Press, 1990], 51) found that a child goes through three stages in learning household tasks. First they need help with the job. Later they need only reminding or supervision. Finally they do their jobs without reminding or supervision.

For instance, a child can begin cooking a meal at age seven. At about age nine, he or she can cook the meal but requires supervision. At thirteen a properly trained child should be able to cook a meal alone for the most part.

Crary found that some jobs follow a little different pattern. A five- to eleven-year-old needs help vacuuming. At eleven children should be independent. However, at about twelve they may need supervision again because they get careless.

A nine-year-old can do laundry with help. In about four years, they are almost independent. At fourteen they should be able to vacuum completely on their own.

Obviously these ages vary with children's learning ability and the parent's teaching skills. However the patterns are the same.

The consequences you set up are part of the supervision you give. Verbal reminding has a limited place because you don't want the child to become dependent on your verbal prompting (and prompting, and more prompting). That will become nagging, which nobody likes. Keep your goal in mind. You are building children who act in a responsible way. You are aiming for adults who are capable and can be counted on—in short, a person of excellence.

That's why you don't want to revert to just using your reminders to get the job done. You need to follow through dispassionately with your plan—that they will consistently do certain jobs. Don't express disappointment, cajole, or the like when they falter. Just follow through with the built-in consequences every time.

All moms will be tempted to relent when Bill starts running out of clothes. They will want to give him another chance, to quit when their husband suggests they are being too harsh. You will need to regroup with your husband if this starts to happen. Giving in at this point will undermine the process and put you back where you started. Be firm with your children.

Why You May Feel Stalled

If you are reading this book, you have already made a move toward changing the way you keep house. Maybe you have been motivated to do things differently but somehow you just can't get going. We'll consider a few reasons why this may be true.

Chronically Overextended

Sometimes the Manager-mom has gotten to the point where she has committed herself beyond her store of energy. Someone looking at her life would marvel at how much she is trying to accomplish. She may be raising a large family, working outside the home, home schooling, taking care of elderly relatives, or helping her husband with his business.

Like a Slinky toy that has been overstretched, she doesn't have any resiliency left. She starts tolerating clutter, slipping on daily maintenance jobs, letting dishes soak in the sink longer than makes sense, failing to pick up things dropped on the floor, and often misplacing things.

The kids are available but she can't rally herself enough to get them going and supervise them. Zombielike, she does the bare minimum and sogs through day after day, coming up occasionally to look around and wonder why she is so "lazy."

She fought the house and the house won. Stress has worn her out, and the house has been a big part of that stress. She and all her soul sisters who have too much to do need to step back, take a deep breath, unload the less important jobs, and focus only on a few important priorities in life. Slowly, she will regain her equilibrium and be able to manage again.

Later, when there is less to do and the kids are older, overextended moms who have had to cut back on activities can begin to add those things that have been previously thinned out. Life's very busy times do not last forever and today's life expectancy is long. There is more time than you think to do the things that lure you into overactivity.

Really Depressed

Depression puts the brakes on productivity. This condition, often undiagnosed, paralyzes both thinking and movement, so that doing the simplest things seems like a very big deal.

When Mom is depressed, she is not able to face the demands of parenthood. Jen complained of her "runaway" four year old who was a one-girl tornado. Six months later Jen reported that things got better when she received treatment for depression. Then she was able to devise a plan for taming her tornado. When she followed it consistently and gently, things began to turn around. Not that they are perfect but much better.

Related to the problem of depression is the drag on a woman's life from problems such as ill relatives, the children's school problems, employment issues, husband-wife friction, and the myriad of "slings and arrows of outrageous fortune that flesh is heir to."

Really Tired

Women often complain of fatigue. Overcommitted, overworked, and overstressed, anybody who does as much as most women do has good reason to be tired.

However, sometimes that tiredness is not because Mom is doing too much. It may have a physical cause such as hypoglycemia, thyroid dysfunction, poor diet, mononucleosis, untreated diabetes, poor sleep habits, allergies, fibromyalgia, chronic fatigue syndrome, or a number of other causes. Many of these are found more commonly in women.

These conditions require competent medical help—someone who will give the symptom of "tiredness" the attention it needs.

Hidden Baggage

Mom does not come to the management task without any baggage of her own. Most of the time, the thoughtful mom can spot and handle her own problems.

On occasion these have a deeper psychological cause and require outside help.

One condition that has often been overlooked is attention deficit disorder in adults. According to Dale Jordan in his book *Attention Deficit Disorder,* disorganization is the "earmark" of this malady. Sari Solden pays particular attention to this in her book, *Attention Deficit Disorder in Women: Embracing Disorganization at Home and in the Workplace* (Grass Valley: Underwood Books, 1995) in which she states, "Disorganization in one form or another is the subject that most women with ADD talk about the most in counseling either:

- the stress of living with it,
- strategies for dealing with it,
- or the emotions surrounding it."

When a mom is distractible and has difficulty focusing on her goals for the house and the kids to boot, she will consistently experience difficulty. As she flits from one unfinished task to another, she often has no clue as to what she is doing differently from those who are successful.

In addition to ADD, hardworking moms who sincerely want to do their best for their families sometimes are struggling with hidden issues such as bipolar disorder, an obsessive-compulsive tendency to hoard, or some other issues that should be addressed professionally before these moms will be able to fulfill their dreams.

Overwhelmed

Some moms don't naturally rise to the challenge of the kids' resistance. They allow the children to spiral out of control. They may be nice kids. Mom may be a nice lady; Dad, a nice guy. But the dynamics have gotten so offtrack that the parents have lost control. It shows up in this whole housekeeping thing. Mom needs to face her helplessness and learn how she can get control back. The kids need a mom who can handle the job she has been given.

Where the Buck Stops

To our surprise, the hardest person to manage is often the one whose picture is on our driver's license. The condition of the house right now is what we have made it. If we are overworked and harried, it is because we chose to go that way. We may not have done it intentionally, but small decision by small decision and in every important way, it is our doing. Without meaning to, we have built in attitudes, circumstances, and habits that are incrementally and consistently taking us down into this mess.

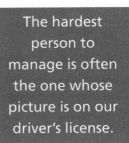

The hardest person to manage is often the one whose picture is on our driver's license.

If we have any hope of changing our house, family, and children, we must first change ourselves. Most of the books in the Messie series (*The New Messies Manual, Messie No More, Messies Superguide,* and *Meditations for Messies*) deal with this very issue. *When You Live with a Messie* deals with other adults who are heavy contributors to the problem. It is a big subject. Read these or other books to get on the road to successful self-management. Look for hindrances you may be living with, including some we have already considered.

- You may find that deep down you are afraid to have a neat and organized house because you would feel unneeded.

- You may feel uncomfortable with order in the home because you have grown used to the mess.
- You may be afraid to delegate because that would change family dynamics.
- You may be using your house as an excuse to withdraw from stressful social occasions.
- Perhaps you are just not in really good health for any number of reasons that need addressing. You are neglecting yourself and your health.
- Possibly you don't know how to organize or delegate because you have never learned.

Whatever the problem, the answer lies with you. There is no getting around it. The buck for the house stops at the desk of the "woman of the house."

Rosalie's Response

We met in my backyard on the patio, overlooking the native plants my husband had planted to attract the birds and butterflies that call the southern tip of Florida home. Large red glasses of iced tea cast a rosy glow on the green patio table as we talked. It was early spring, still cool enough to enjoy the outdoors. Summer was coming, when the heat and humidity would force us into the air-conditioned indoors.

"I've already seen some of the things you mentioned in myself," said Rosalie. "When you start to change, you begin to notice things in your life that you didn't even know were there before.

"Let me show you an insight that a woman in one of my Internet groups had because of something that happened. It's rather long. I could tell you about it but she says it so well."

Rosalie handed me a computer printout and sipped her tea as I read. A rooster crowed from the yard of one of my neighbors, a common occurrence in Miami. Bees buzzed around the blossoms nearby.

I had a meeting with my daughter's teacher last week. We started to talk, and she suddenly blurted out that I drop by the classroom too often. I was astonished. I thought I was being supportive, bringing things that my daughter forgot in the morning, etc.

She told me that it was disruptive, that I needed to let go, because my daughter IS in 3rd grade, and is ready to separate from me. In the future, if she forgets something, I should just leave it at the office, rather than bring it down to the classroom personally.

I got upset and left, thinking, "I encourage independence in my kids, grumble." Something bothered me about this, though, because I knew she was right, but I didn't know why.

Coincidentally, a short time later while I was doing a questionnaire in a book to assess my problems, to my astonishment, I wrote down, "Disorganization & clutter helps me control my children, and KEEPS THEM DEPENDENT ON ME."

You could have knocked me over with a feather. Evidently, my subconscious had been working overtime after the talk with the teacher.

Not only is MY disorganization passed on to my children as a family style, but I am thwarting their development by limiting their choices of how and when to do things. The way things work in the morning, half the time, there's the mad search for clean clothes, shoes & socks, there are forgotten lunches (or lunches needing to be delivered after the kids go to school because I didn't get them packed), there's the search for the homework, or signatures for the homework, etc.

You can see that a LOT of this results in a whole bunch of "Thanks, Mom!!" And, when I show up at school with "forgotten" things, I'm a big hero, rescuing my kids.

No wonder I take the stuff directly to the classrooms— I get gratitude from my kids directly, and look caring to the other kids and the teachers!! I end up feeling good because I take such good care of my children, when all I'm doing is digging them out of the chaos at home and sending them off for the day to try to conform with the organization at school. Obviously they're getting no support at home, or rather ARE getting support to stay disorganized. I'M AN ENABLER!!!

I've resolved that my goal for the first school quarter will be to truly inspire independence in my kids by setting a priority to keep their "supplies" organized to help them. So they can choose what they will wear (not what happens to be clean that day & isn't too wrinkled). So they can do their homework without hero Mom saving the day with pencils & paper & glue sticks conjured up out of thin air. So they can pack their own backpacks & be responsible for their things, and the independence will carry over to school where they can return their own library books, buy lunch if they forget their bag lunches, and freeze if they don't take their jackets. (I understand from other parents, they only freeze ONCE!)

You know, I think it will be harder for ME than for them.

Looking up, I said, "Umm. Interesting story. She got quite a revelation. It sure changed her management approach."

"Yes," said Rosalie thoughtfully, swirling her ice around in the empty glass. "It was a revelation to me too. I realize from reading this how easy it is to think we are doing one thing and really are doing another. I think it was Pogo who said, 'We have met the enemy, and he is us.' I guess we all have to be on the alert for those hidden thoughts that keep dragging us back into the old way of doing things."

"If you are alert, you will see them," I said. "They become exposed as you begin to change your behavior." Then changing the subject I asked, "Since you are here, would you like to see some of the systems I have set up in my house?"

Rosalie jumped at the chance to look into my house in detail. I took her to the kitchen cabinets and showed her the way I had grouped things together, put them into appropriately sized containers, which were in a logical place for use, and labeled them. I had done the same thing in my utility closet.

"These labels keep me straight," I said. "I have such a tendency to get sucked into disorder that without them, stuff would start to move out of place and get lost. It's necessary for me to do this. Obviously other folks can keep a neat house without going this route. I can't. I guess everybody has to find what works for her."

We went to the clothes closet and I explained how I group my clothes, label the groups, and hang the pieces in each group from light to dark colors. When I showed her my refrigerator, she gasped in surprise, like everybody does, at the food—grouped and stored in plastic baskets with labels on them.

"You've turned your refrigerator into a dresser where you can pull out the containers like drawers!" Rosalie laughed.

"Yep, works for me," I said. "But, what you don't see, Rosalie, are the schedules I have made to keep me on track. You can't see the new habits I have had to develop to counter the disorganization that is always lurking in the wings of my organizational stage. My schedules aren't extensive but they are important

because they are what make these systems work if I
follow them consistently."

Later, as I saw Rosalie to the door, I said, "Next time
let's turn our attention to the family and see how your
vision can be worked out in a practical way in that arena.
I think you are ready to begin formulating your plan."

SIX

Turn the Spotlight on the Family

No problem can stand the assault of sustained thinking.

Voltaire

When we think about how well we're doing being a Manager, our focus is often on the house. We need to turn the spotlight on the family instead. One way to keep the emphasis where it belongs is to have a family motto that ties the family to the house. Obviously you as the mom are going to have to take the lead on developing this motto. Here are several mottoes that emphasize slightly different aspects of the family's goals.

> In our family everybody works.
> We are a team.

Our family does everything necessary
to have a home we can be proud of—
all the time and in every area.
Big job but we can do it!

Good habits, planning, teamwork, communication,
efficiency—our family's formula
for a harmonious house.

Working together, we are committed
to do whatever it takes whenever it takes
to create a house we can be proud of.

It takes family teamwork
to make our family dream work.

When you decide on a motto, have your family memorize it. Put it on the wall, on the mirror, in the bedroom. Review it at breakfast. Cross-stitch it. I would say put it on the lunch boxes, but that may be excessive. Use your own judgment on how to weave the motto into your family's everyday life.

These mottoes apply only to the house. In addition to the house-related motto, many families also develop an overall family motto. Stephen Covey gives information on how to do this in his book, *Seven Habits of a Highly Effective Family* (New York: Golden Books, 1998).

Handle the motto gingerly. Don't make it a dictum that you hold inflexibly over the family's head. The motto is a guide to the family and is best served up with a sense of fun and joy bound together in a loving environment. It should be a part of the essential bonding of family members.

Don't underestimate the importance of having a motto. It keeps the pursuit of your goals from turning into a list of rules that you force down unwilling throats "for your own good." Beating your family over the head with the motto stultifies this whole "noble" cause. Think of the motto as a gift that will serve to bind the family together in a unified effort.

Focus on the Children

As you work with your family, envision the characteristics you want your children to have as adults. These are the ones to be working on today. Let's name a few. We want our children to be:

- hard working—doing his part with zest
- efficient—getting the job done quickly and well
- a good communicator—listening well to instructions and having good input
- responsible—doing what is right without constant supervision
- a self-starter—seeing what needs to be done and doing it
- a good time manager—punctual, doesn't procrastinate
- smart about practicalities—learning what things work and what don't
- respectful of self—thinking he deserves to live a well-ordered life
- respectful of others—thinking of what others want and need
- thoughtful and caring—doing more than his share when the situation requires it

- a good team member—working well with others in every way
- fair—not burdening others with his things or jobs
- positive toward work—having a healthy "can do" mind-set
- self-controlled—saying yes or no to his wants as appropriate

Can you think of a better setting to work on these things than side by side with your child in the house on a daily basis? Modeling and training these characteristics on the job is much better than just talking about them. The talking takes root and is meaningful only as the child is actually doing a job that requires these attributes.

Kid Meets Real World

Someday your child will be facing life situations where he will need to have life skills pretty well mastered in order to function with dignity and efficiency. The time for your child to learn these skills is while he is with you. If you do your job right, by the time the child is fourteen or so, he should be able to manage the house on a basic level if you should be away from the home for a while. By sixteen, he should be able to do it well.

Imagine you are away from home to care for a sick relative, have a hospital stay, or go on vacation. Because you have trained your children, you know that when you return, the house will be in good condition. But better than that, you know that while you are gone, the family was well cared for because they know how to do all the tasks necessary for their comfort and well-being.

And they have the skills and the mental characteristics that encourage them to do a good job.

Brett tells that he and his two brothers used to get home from school before his single mom returned from work. Their habit was to have the house cleaned and in order and dinner in the oven when she arrived home.

For the boys to do this was not a big undertaking. Two guys can pick up, vacuum, clean the bathrooms, or whatever on a rotating planned basis for half an hour a day and keep the house in good shape.

> The talking takes root and is meaning-ful only as the child is actually doing a job that requires these attributes.

Another can put the meal on with twenty or thirty minutes' preparation time and have it in the oven smelling good when Mom gets home. Dinner may be baked chicken and baked potatoes with a canned vegetable, prewashed salad greens, and hot store-bought rolls, or frozen, family-sized lasagna from the super market with added fixings. None of this is hard work. All it requires is training, a can-do attitude, and a desire to make a responsible contribution to the family, especially to Mom.

By the way, when telling this story Brett expressed a great deal of gratitude to his mom for the hard work she had done supporting the family. He also said that he had maintained a lifelong love of cooking. It had become an enjoyable hobby for him in his adult years.

How different this story is from the ones I hear from moms who come home from work later than their teens and find that the house they left orderly is now a shambles! They have eight more hours of work to do—and lots of exhausting yelling to boot.

I recall particularly the story of a Midwest mother who spent the day on the tractor until late afternoon during the summer growing season. When she came into the house, exhausted after a very long day in the fields, she would find the house wrecked by the two teenage sons whom she had left in the house to care for her younger son while she was in the field. I suppose the reason I remember it so clearly was her frustrated and desperate tone as she told her story. Their lack of appreciation and caring had hurt her far more than the mess itself.

The Strong-Willed, Uncooperative Child

At this point it is important to acknowledge that in some cases other childhood issues are of such overriding importance that neatness is the least of the Manager-mom's problems. One of these is dealing with strong-willed children.

Doing research on strong-willed children, Dr. James Dobson conducted a study of 35,000 parents. He discovered that about 21 percent of children can be categorized as very strong-willed. Another 13 percent are somewhat strong-willed. Putting these two groups together adds up to about a third of children whose natural tendency is to resist instruction. These are difficult children to raise. If you are dealing with a child of this nature, do yourself the favor of reading Dobson's *Parenting Isn't for Cowards*, which deals with this subject. Run, don't walk, to the bookstore to get other books listed on pages 227 and 228 for further help. You owe it to yourself and your child. Without the understanding you get from such books, you will become extremely frustrated and unnecessarily guilt ridden.

A mom dealing with one of these exceedingly strong-willed children who challenges her on every issue, a child with uncontrolled ADD, one suffering clinical depression, or one with any other basic problem that seriously affects normal functioning must address these problems as the primary issue before taking on the neatness issue. In these cases, Mom will settle for survival. Even when dealing with these long-term issues, the house can't be totally ignored, but it may need to take a distant second place.

Three Important Issues for Growth

For the ordinary child, however, working on the neatness issue can play an important part in his or her maturity. Unless the child is included as an integral part of the housework in both keeping his room organized and helping out with the rest of the house, he may fail to learn three important concepts. By expecting the child to take his place in household maintenance, we say three important things to that child:

- *You are an important team member.* Experts suggest that being included in the practical functioning of the home with chores builds confidence in the child that he is an important person in the life of the family.
- *The family is a priority.* Chris Evert, champion tennis player, says her parents were the greatest at helping her keep her feet on the ground in the midst of fame. To illustrate, she related that when she returned a hero from England where she had won at Wimbledon, she was immediately expected to do her part of the family chores by folding laundry.

If we allow our children to cop out of chores just because they have sports, study, parties, or Wimbledon to win, we are telling them that these things take priority over the family. When they become adults, what will be priorities for them—work and other interests or home and family?

- *Having a neat house and room is important.* It is understandable that sometimes children go through stages when they are busier than at other times and they have trouble making a strong contribution to the family. Kevin Leman, author of *Making Children Mind without Losing Yours* (rev. ed., Revell, 2000), believes children should be given reduced responsibilities in the home during the teen years because of the heavy drain on their time by school work, extracurricular activities, and sometimes a job. Even then, however, they should be included to a reasonable extent.

Once children are included in the family plan, they should be expected to take that responsibility seriously. Don't let sympathy undermine your expectation that they are responsible for getting their jobs done, whether they do them themselves, pay another family member to do them, or trade off with somebody else. The point is, whatever the circumstance, they are responsible.

A lot of other factors that are a part of life may come into play with teens. Sometimes basically neat kids will experiment with the Messie lifestyle for a while to gauge their own comfort zone. Occasionally children who have not seemed to care about neatness while at home kick into a whole different mode when they get their own place. Then they take ownership of the situation. Even so, it's not a good idea to let teens cop out of their responsibilities, whether we expect they will improve later or not.

Obviously being flexible is necessary, but don't let down on the important concept of your having an organized and beautiful home for yourself and your family when the children are in the house. You can't let the condition of your home depend on the understanding of an immature young person.

I can think of no other activity that draws the family together as a team on a day by day, month by month, year by year basis as working together to keep a clean and orderly house. We can learn details about our children as we work with them, details we might miss otherwise. We can spot ups and downs. We can reinforce our leadership position.

One mom assigned a one-week stint for each child to help her with cleaning up in the kitchen after dinner. She not only taught cleanup skills, she also had a chance to relate on a personal basis as she worked with each child. Boys especially prefer talking while working to having a face-to-face interaction.

Working side by side, we can converse about a variety of important topics, such as homework, telling the truth, getting along with siblings, sharing, not whining, and the like. We can reinforce good behavior and our personal relation with the child by slipping in compliments and praise. Done right, we can build bridges when we work together.

One important emphasis of this book is getting the kids to keep their rooms in order and become responsible team members in the household management project. But it doesn't stop there. The life lessons we are teaching our children apply in many areas of discipline and training. Slowly, line upon line, precept upon precept, here a little, there a little, mature personalities are formed.

A Picture of Maturity

It is useful to concentrate on the positive side of the picture. In his book *Parenting Isn't for Cowards,* Dr.

James Dobson investigates the qualities of the compliant child. This child is not a weak-willed wimp. For the most part he is easy to get along with because of qualities such as self-control, obedience, focus on the needs of others, willingness to share power appropriately, and the like. Of course, the compliant child is not an angel (who is?), and not all children in this category are equally compliant.

Because of these characteristics, when these children become adults, they tend to be successful in their careers, relationships, and other important aspects of their lives. They are the kind of people we all enjoy having as friends. They think of us, are proactive in meeting our needs, and offer thoughtful counsel. When they have a responsibility, we can count on them to fulfill it. When they have important decisions to make, they seek advice from wise sources. Because they don't have to spend time cleaning up messes they make in their own lives, they can contribute creatively to the lives of others.

A person who is driving his wife crazy by making messes or not paying bills because they are lost does not fit into this picture of maturity. Many otherwise mature and creative adults have cluttered homes. Obviously, for their sakes and yours, they need to mature in that area as well.

While these characteristics of maturity come more naturally to some children than others, it is our job as parents to do our best to foster them in all of our children. Working together to accomplish our family goal is only one part of a whole array of ways we do this.

Keep a daily vision of your son or daughter as a capable, mature adult. Hold on to it even in the midst of the turmoil of family life, childhood complaints, and parental discouragements. Those ever-present chores will still need to be done. In the long run, they will be done better, more smoothly, with better flow when they are done in conjunction with your child-development plan.

What Really Works

When moving our kids into maturity, we need expert help. Children respond to different approaches as they grow and change. The stages of maturity are outlined by Drs. Henry Cloud and John Townsend in their enlightening book *Boundaries with Kids*. They suggest love first and setting limits with consequences second. They describe the developmental stages of maturity as follows:

- *Fear of consequences.* As you set limits, your child's earliest cooperative response will be because of fear of consequences. We must set appropriate limits and deliver consequences fairly and unemotionally. Even as adults, we respond to traffic laws partly because we don't want to get a ticket. However, we hope that our child will move beyond this to a more internalized reason for doing the right thing.
- *Immature conscience.* Eventually the child will begin to internalize the parent's voice to some extent. At the appropriate time, his brain will tell him, "Boys who are neat lift the seat." Or when she is debating whether or not to hang up her coat, she will hear her mother's voice in her head repeating the thirty-second rule, "If it takes thirty seconds or less to do, do it immediately."
- *Values and ethics.* After a while the child begins to appropriate what he has learned at the other levels. He begins to question whether things are right or wrong as new choices arise.

He asks the following questions:

> Is a neat house really important?
> How should I use my time?
> What is my responsibility to the family?

- *Mature love and mature guilt.* As the child develops a sensitivity to others and comes to believe that he is accountable to God for his actions, he makes decisions and choices based on these concerns. These are internalized boundaries.

  Now the internal dialog, sometimes subliminal, may go something like this:

> Mom has worked hard. It is not fair for me to make a mess for her to clean up. Clutter in my room interferes with God's plan for my life. Order and beauty are their own reward. I want to be ready to be a contributing member of the family I set up.

We need to be aware that the child may be developing unevenly in several of these levels at the same time. A child may be grappling with the complex problem of right and wrong on one level and yet need to be reminded about simple consequences on another, all at one time.

We are working to bring the child to the point where he does not clutter because he has a maturing outlook. It may be because she wants a lovely house herself or because he wants to make things easier for his mom or because she is a team player working with the family to create the home the family wants. The child is moving beyond behaving properly just so he will not be punished for messing things up.

Sigmund Freud once defined the nature of maturity in two words, *working* and *loving*. There is much to what he said at this point. Raising a child to adulthood who is responsible in work and able to maintain loving relationships takes a lot of time, training, attention, patience, and vision. That's what this is all about. Is it worth it? You betcha it is.

The Father Factor

In this book, heavy emphasis has been placed on the place of Mom in getting and keeping the organization of the house under control. Don't get the wrong idea. The fact that this book is directed to Mom does not mean that Dad does not have a very important part to play in determining the condition of the house. His place has often been wrongfully overlooked by society. More and more, this is changing. When parents are initiating a new approach to the organization of the home, kids need united direction, example, and supervision from both Mom and Dad. Mom needs Dad's encouragement and support in her efforts. In the best of all worlds, Dad would be involved in keeping the home team working together in the house as in all aspects of family life.

But sometimes Dad does not take his place as a leader in organizing and does not share Mom's concern for upgrading the condition of the house. He may drop things when he comes in, fail to share chores, and the like. If he is a part of the problem, that is serious indeed and needs to be faced by the woman who not only has messy kids but also a messy husband. Her managerial skills will be tested to the max. The last thing she needs or wants is to be the mom to a grown man. My book *When You Live with a Messie* deals in depth with this problem.

The Windows Are Closing

The brain of a child is not just an untrained adultlike brain. It has a different configuration and is constantly changing as the child grows. During childhood and until as late as the early twenties, the brain is developing in specific areas on a set schedule. As different areas develop, new skills can be taught that the child was not fully ready to learn before. What is not so well-known is that the optimum times for learning certain skills are also closing down as these changes occur.

During these optimum times, skills can be hardwired into the brain in a way they can never be later. As children develop, they can learn organizational skills that will become an integral part of their personalities and serve them for the rest of their lives. Like every other skill, organizational skills are easier for some children to learn than for others, but all need to learn to the best of their ability. Organization is the track on which every aspect of life moves forward. To neglect this training, for whatever reason, is to do a great disservice to the child for the rest of his life.

> To neglect teaching organizational skills is to do a great disservice to the child for the rest of his life.

The windows of opportunity are closing. Although it is easiest for children to learn during these optimum times, they can if they try very hard as I did, learn as adults to build systems in which they can organize themselves. But it will never come as naturally, or work as well, as for the person who lays down those organizational tracks in childhood.

Rosalie's Response

We met at an East Indian restaurant midway between our houses on Rosalie's day off. We chose to have lunch there because of its quiet atmosphere. Exotic fabrics and paintings surrounded us as we sat in a booth against a wall made of filigreed wood. A few patrons sat talking at tables in the small room.

Rosalie looked more relaxed than I had seen her as she chose the hottest curry. I took what was a bold step for me and ordered the medium-hot curry.

"I don't think they make food as spicy for women as for men. Ben and I ordered the same spicy dish at a Thai restaurant and his was much hotter than mine," Rosalie said.

I secretly hoped this might be so as I was feeling nervous about my choice.

"What does Ben think about the changes you are making around the house?" I asked as we waited for our meal.

"Well, Ben has come on board with this whole project. I'm grateful he is not uncooperative when it comes to making changes like the husband of this woman in our group on the Internet. That would make things so much harder."

She handed me a printout that read:

I say in all honesty my sanity depends on getting my house together. My kids have never lived in a cleaned-up environment. They have no idea what it takes to have a nice home. Part of my problem is that my husband never learned that as a child. His mother did EVERYTHING for them. Now I am raising sons and a daughter who will be just as bad as their father in that respect. They are wonderful children in every other way. The time has come for them to learn what it takes to live like normal people do.

"This e-mail reminds me that I sure don't want my kids to grow up and be the problem to their spouses that this guy is. It's a scary thing to think about." Rosalie frowned as she talked but then she smiled widely as she said, "We've had a family meeting already and chosen a motto! It is a Latin statement that means 'Seek to excel!' It means that our family will work together to build a life of excellence. Right now we are focusing on the house, but it has applications in other areas too. Ben wanted it to be in Greek because that was what he learned in seminary. Because nobody could pronounce or even read the Greek letters, he was outvoted. Becky is finishing her second year of Latin in high school. She has a flair for the dramatic so this motto was her suggestion. The twins like it too. They want to get together some ideas for a family crest for our next meeting. We are talking about making T-shirts with our crest and motto on them to wear when we have special family meetings or get-togethers."

"Wow! You've taken off at a gallop! Do you think you might be going pretty fast on this thing?"

"Well, I'm just a new Manager and I don't exactly know what I am doing," she said, laughing a little. And then more seriously she added, "I hope I'm not starting out at a sprint and will wear myself out. I realize this is a marathon, a marathon for life, really.

"But I thought we needed something to draw us together, and I was thrilled with their involvement. Of course I suspect they will want to let the motto and the T-shirts with the crest substitute for the everyday household activities. It will be my job to keep the enthusiasm up and to translate it into real-life accomplishment."

Rosalie told of her plans to have people over more often, which would please her husband. It would also keep them on their toes to keep the house orderly so they wouldn't have to wear themselves out for guests. She spoke of the possibility of getting some household help occasionally if the budget would allow. The kids would look at their rooms in a different light if they knew somebody else was going in to clean their bedrooms. She had great confidence that this combination of things, especially using the family motto, would make a big improvement.

"You're right in believing that people will work hard to accomplish a new goal but have little enthusiasm for solving old problems. But remember, this is all new to them. It's new to you too. Move forward steadily but carefully."

After we finished our meal, I felt the need of a cool, yogurt drink, and Rosalie ordered chai, a spicy, sweet, milk-based hot tea.

"You know," she said, "I think I've begun to see how this all fits together. For the first time, I'm understanding the importance of vision, family teamwork, and all of the other principles you've been talking about. But, you know what? I've got a real problem with the condition of the house. I was amazed at what you showed me you have done with your place. I can see I might straighten up my family but now I have to go back and rescue my house from the disorder that has developed over the years."

I agreed with Rosalie that it was time to discuss the house. What she had seen at my house worked when it was applied to me but was not necessarily for her. I needed to explain the principles of what she had seen and encourage her to apply them to her house in a way that made sense to her for her situation. I encouraged Rosalie to involve her family in the dejunking and reorganizing of the house, which would be an invaluable lesson for the children in how to organize a house from the beginning. If they worked with her to get it in shape, they would have a vested interest in keeping it that way.

Idea 10
The house must be prepared to cooperate with your plans.

"However," I pointed out, "you will have to be the leader in this project because there are a lot of organizational decisions to be made. Include other family members wherever you can, especially when you are dealing with their rooms.

"So, next time, we talk about the house."

SEVEN

Managing the Runaway House

"If a guy has a messy apartment, he's just your typical bachelor. But if a girl has a messy apartment, she's branded a slob."

Character in *Snagged,* Carol Higgins Clark

Once you see the importance of putting on your managerial hat and are getting ready to begin a new way of approaching the problem of keeping the house in order, you will notice that the first obvious obstacle is the condition of the house. It is not ready for your managed family to function successfully.

Your Vision for the House

Now is the time to turn your attention to your dream for the house. What is that dream? If you could wave a wand and magically turn your house into your dream home, what would that house be like?

Maybe you are afraid to try to dream because it seems so impossible. Or maybe you have been under the pressure of clutter for so long, your vision has been squeezed out of your consciousness. Possibly you may be tempted to take a utilitarian view and feel that how the house looks is not important as long as it works okay.

Somewhere, somehow, you are going to have to find a dream that is so powerful, so wonderful, so inspiring that it will carry you forward even in the most difficult times. The Visionary part of your personality will stabilize you as you strive to bring the house into the kind of order it needs to function as you like.

Let us remember again that our goal is not just to get rid of clutter. The end goal is to create a home of harmony, order, and beauty. To do that, steps must be taken to get the house organized so it will cooperate with us in accomplishing our ultimate goal.

Three Steps to Order

The three steps that we will follow to whip the house into shape are explained in more detail in *The New Messies Manual*. When you and your family can locate things easily *and* can get them out and put them back with very little effort, your house is ready for your managing techniques to work.

Use the three S's to get your act together: simplify, sort, store.

Simplify

One of the chief differences between people who struggle unsuccessfully with organizing and those who organize easily is how much stuff they keep. Disorganized people keep too much stuff because they are sentimental, because they think they might need things in the future, and because the things they keep give them comfort and define their personalities.

An Internet mom explained her insight:

> I discovered too that we can organize until we're blue in the face, but it doesn't help. . . . it's the "stuff" that's the problem. I got rid of tons of stuff at my garage sale this summer, made many trips to Salvation Army also, and continue to do so. I can't say how happy it makes me feel to open my closet and find bare space on the shelf!!!

Here is a short explanation of a dejunking system called the Mount Vernon method, which was adapted from a system used for cleaning at George Washington's home. The Mount Vernon method isn't about cleaning. It is basic decluttering and organizing.

One Messie explained it to another this way:

> With the Mount Vernon method, you pick the drawer or closet closest to your front door and you begin to chuck the stuff that you no longer need. You begin to divorce yourself from junk. It is SCARY for a pack-rat like me. The Mount Vernon method takes months, literally, because you're doing it like you would eat an elephant: one bite at a time. You do one drawer a day or a week or whatever you can face.
>
> But it's like dieting: You have to change your whole mindset. If you clean out a drawer, you have to enjoy the lovely feeling of it being EMPTY and keep it that way. For most Messies, if it comes in the front door, junk tends to stay in the house.
>
> Once you start at the front door and inch around the periphery of each room emptying drawers, nooks, cran-

nies, cupboards, and the like until you get back to the front door your house will be basically dejunked.

The children's rooms are among the most important to dejunk. Outgrown clothes, broken and deserted toys, and a myriad of other kid related items need to be evaluated. Those that are not needed by the child in that room must be removed. If they are being saved for the next children in line, they need to be put in storage.

Sort

After you have gotten rid of the excess, everything that is left *must* be gathered into like groups. That is, you should have a tool area, a wrapping center, a first-aid center, and the like. The center, or zone, may just be a designated spot on the shelf. All houses, large or small, must have designated grouping areas. The same must be done with the children's things. Like things must be grouped together. All Legos, all of Barbie paraphernalia, all hair scrunchies, and the like. Only by establishing designated centers can you build order into your house.

Store

Once you have your belongings pared down to just a few things, which you have sorted into groups, you need to store these things in a way that works easily so that you and your family have no excuse for not finding, retrieving, and putting back any item in the house, including toys. If your storage does not allow for easy access, nobody will use it. Essentially that means you put each grouping in a container that is the proper size to hold the items in that group.

Often, people leave things out in visible piles because they like to assure themselves that their belongings are indeed "there." For that reason it is best to buy an open topped plastic basket or box that makes the items easy to see.

Next, put an easily visible label on the front of the box or basket. Write the label in large letters with a bold marker. For children, a picture along with the word will tell them where something is stored and where to return it.

Finally, the container should be put within easy reach if it is often used. If it is seldom used, put it in a less accessible spot. Now the house is ready to cooperate and support you as you employ your emerging managerial skills.

The Flipper System

Okay, you've got your vision! You've addressed your own personal issues and dealt with them. You're working on new habits. You've got the house under control. Now what else do you do about getting those wheels on the road and moving forward? You set in place a systematic pattern, such as the one provided by the Flipper system or some other schedule system.

To make a Flipper you do the following: First, obtain a photo album with plastic sleeves that flip down in a staggered fashion over each other. Each of these plastic sleeves holds a card on which to write chores for one day of the week. There is usually enough room for four weeks' worth of chores. The plastic sleeves hold the cards in their place in the week so we can flip through them in order day after day. Some jobs need to be done more often than others, of course, so they will be put down several times during the month on several days. Some, perhaps bill paying, will only need to be put on a card once or twice during a month. The Flipper method is explained in more detail in *The New Messies Manual.* Here's how one recovering disorganized mom explained the Flipper on the web site (www.Messies .com) to another mom who was selling her house and was afraid of being embarrassed by the real estate salesman's unexpected visits.

> The Flipper method is how you deal with day-to-day surface clutter. The Flipper method is a way to face your housecleaning. You shouldn't have to deep clean every day; the Lord didn't mean for you to. The first question you have to ask is "What makes my house look clean and company-ready?" If you can define what state your house would have to be in for you not to cringe at the sight of guests coming up the front walk, you're on your way.
>
> I decided what would make my house company-ready. If the beds are made, the dishes washed, the floors swept every day and mopped weekly, the carpet vacuumed weekly, the clothes washed, the bathrooms clean, and the furniture dusted, then it's clean.
>
> Now, divide those duties over the span of a week. I do a few things (very few) every day. I do other things just once a week (wash clothes, mop, vacuum, clean bathrooms). If you keep to your schedule, it doesn't matter if the real estate guy comes in at midnight—you'll not be embarrassed. And since you'll want to keep to the same basic schedule in your new house when you move, why not start now and reap the benefits? You probably won't even have to change your Flipper.

Change Habits

At this point many people race to make a chart for chores, both theirs and the kids. That is not where the solution lies. The solution is in changing regular, everyday, ingrained, unproductive habits. Some might call them "lazy" habits.

How can you and your family change your habits? This is a huge question! The answers are deceptively simple. There are three rules to follow. Get your family to follow them, and your house will be transformed.

> The solution is in changing regular, everyday, ingrained, unproductive habits.

- *Honor the sanctity of the family areas and your bedroom.* Your living room cannot double as an office or clothes-folding area nor your dining room as a storage area. These rooms are the canvas on which you paint the dreams of your home. Allow no alien belongings to be dropped there—even for "just a minute" or "so I'll remember them."

  Occasionally you may fold clothes or do paper-work in these areas, but the clothes and papers may be allowed there only when you are working with them. When you leave the area, they go with you.

- *Use the camper's rule.* Leave the area the same as or better than you found it.

- *Follow the thirty second rule.* If it takes thirty seconds or less to accomplish the job, don't put it off. Do it right away.

Habits are hard to break. New habits are hard to create. But if you really care enough about changing the condition of the whole house, including the children's rooms, you will build these new habits into your life.

Some of your friends never struggle with their houses because they know the secrets of maintaining an orderly home. These three rules are the secrets that your friends know. Because they follow these rules, their houses look nice even without their working at it. You can drop over any time and their houses look good. Consistently applied, these rules will change your life.

Four Hot Spots

There are four important household tasks that are universally chronic problems: laundry, washing dishes, caring for papers and bills, caring for pets. Solve your problems with these and you may never struggle to maintain an orderly life again. Begin by dividing up the jobs in these four areas among your family members, and proactively address any hitch that seems to interfere with completing these jobs.

1. *Laundry.* Washing the clothes is usually not the problem. Most people do that part easily once the other problems relating to the laundry are solved. Getting the laundry done completely is often a problem because there's too much, it has to be sorted, and it has to be folded and put away.

> Problem: Too much laundry.
> Possible solution: Wear clothes for longer periods of time.
> Possible solution: Keep a hamper in each room and have each person (if they are old enough) launder their own clothes.
>
> Problem: Sorting laundry.
> Possible solution: Have a hamper for each laundry category—colors, whites, towels, and so on.
> Possible solution: Just mix all laundry and wash it all in cold water.

Problem: Folding and putting laundry away
Possible solution: Do one small load daily, including the folding and putting away. Never put folded clothes in a basket because they tend to get stuck there. Take them immediately to where they belong. Do not put another load in the washer until the preceding load is folded and put away.

2. *Dishes.* Dishwashers must be unloaded speedily for any system to work. Dirty stuff begins to back up in the sink or on the counter if the dishwasher has clean dishes in it.
    Possible solution: Follow a schedule. Wash dishes each night whether the dishwasher is full or not; unload each morning or later that night. Train your family to put dishes directly into the dishwasher as they are used during the day.
    Possible solution: Cut down on the number of dishes used. Color code your glasses so each person uses only one glass all day long. Use paper plates regularly. Wash, wipe, and put away your cooking pots and pans as you cook.
3. *Papers and bills.* Papers require decisions and action. That is why they pile up. This is the only job that is primarily an adult responsibility. All of the other jobs can be partially or entirely handled by children. Put the papers and bills waiting for attention into a special folder or a designated drawer. Many like to schedule a day or two a month, usually the first and fifteenth, to pay these bills.
4. *Pets.* Kids usually start their responsibilities by taking care of pets. This job is pretty much a no-brainer. As with all chores, don't expect the kids to do it without supervision, especially when they

first start (and later on for that matter). Just because they have the skill to do a job does not mean they have developed the responsibility. You will need to set and follow specific consequences such as: You don't eat until Spot does.

An Imperceptible Difference

Slowly and surely, things will change. Nonetheless, there will be times when things may regress to looking pretty much the same. The kids may drag out a lot of stuff, or you may get in a time crunch and the house shows it. But in your mind, you will know it is not the same because it is not out of control in the same way it used to be.

When things have gotten out of hand and the house is a mess, you need an emergency approach that will resuscitate it fast and bring it back from the brink!

Here's the system that we call the Mt. Vesuvius system, named for the power of that famous volcano, because we need that kind of surge to make a quick change. Here's what to do:

Buy a banker's box for each member of the family and several extras for miscellaneous items. These are about 12 inches by 18 inches, white with detachable lids, and found in office supply stores. They were designed to hold files for bankers. Label each box in large letters. Put them in the middle of a common area, like living room, family room, kitchen.

Get your family together for this project. This will take less time than you think. Energy is the key. Have a good reward set up for when the job is done.

Have family members run around the room and put their left-out stuff in their boxes and put the top on the box. They should put any papers that belong to them in a file folder in the box. Then they scurry into their rooms and put their stuff away.

If it's impossible to follow this procedure because things are too chaotic in the common area, use a variation of this idea. Obtain more white boxes in addition to the family members' boxes. Label them as suggested below. Pool your family energy—work together.

To make it easier, set the timer for a certain length of time, maybe fifteen minutes. Take a break. Make some kind of change in picking up (maybe switch rooms) and set out on another fifteen-minute stint.

Have a special box for miscellaneous family papers. Save out any bills or checks you come across. Put them in a special area of the house or in a special folder in the box. Label it IMPORTANT PAPERS.

You will find a lot of general house stuff like scissors, coat hangers, laundry (folded and not), toilet paper rolls, left-out groceries, and the like. Have a box for rooms, like KITCHEN, BATHROOM, and BASEMENT. Ferry those to where they belong. Empty them ASAP.

Now the house looks much better. This method leaves a lot of problems unsolved, like when you are going to unload the kitchen, bathroom, and miscellaneous boxes. But in an emergency, it can't be beat for a quick fix.

When there is time to catch up, you can do it. Because your house has a place for things, because your habits have changed, because your family has bought into the project, and because you have a feeling of power over the house, you don't feel panicky or hopeless. Step by step, you systematically regain control and order is restored.

Rosalie's Response

I met Rosalie at her house again. It had been some time since we had met there. The living room was definitely tidy, and I noticed some decorative touches here and there. My eyes followed her into what appeared to be an orderly kitchen as she went to get some coffee and apple pie.

"This is low-cal pie," she said, winking.

"It sure doesn't taste low-cal," I said, enjoying the flaky crust and the juicy filling. "For you, just this one time, I'll make a happy exception about rich desserts! Now tell me how things are going with your organizing project."

"Well, it's been interesting. When I finally tuned into your ideas about habits, I began to see postings on the groups I belong to that I would probably not have realized were so important if you hadn't made it so plain. The first one is really inspiring! It mentions the thirty second rule you say is so important," she said, handing me two printouts from her computer. "That rule must really get around."

"Well, I'm doing my best to spread it," I said. "But I didn't make it up. It is one of the organizing pillars."

The first paper read:

It never ceases to amaze me that my 84-year-old grandmother can still keep a huge home absolutely spotless. When I go to her house in Germany, I try and watch her for clues to how to do it, but she spends so much time waiting on me that I can't see her doing much else. Except, she wipes the kitchen counters after each use, bends to pick up stuff on the carpet when she sees it, wipes up each spill as it happens, etc. So that keeping the house clean seems almost effortless!

Then I started to think about it. Why don't I just follow what my grandmother does and save myself a lot of effort? Because I procrastinate until later, because I think it will take so long and then all those 30 second things become minute things and those minute things become hour things, etc. And pretty soon I have to spend days doing heavy, disgusting cleaning and I end up working a lot harder than my grandmother does with less than half the results.

So, I'm going to take up this cause. I'm going to join ya'll in doing jobs that will take 30 seconds. I'm going to try and clean up after myself as I go along.

Explaining her managing approach, another woman wrote:

The only thing I can even offer here with my son is every night we pick up all his toys from the living room. We sing happy songs, you know, the Barney song clean up, and we do it. I tell him you just have to do it. Then I praise him heavily! Also when we do his room, I sit on the futon and tell him to pick up one thing, put it away. Great. Pick up one thing, put it away. I don't do it for him, I make him do it. He's 5. I don't make this a consistent habit, which I should nightly. He has surprised me a time or two by cleaning his room all by himself without my knowledge! And I could tell he was pleased.

I think with kids, they might not see the importance of it all. They have to want to see it as a good thing. That's what's tricky.

"These both hit a lot of important points," I said, returning the papers.

I had not been in Rosalie's house in some time. I continued to notice changes. Maybe the biggest one was in Rosalie. I had never seen her so relaxed.

When I commented on it, she said, "I used to be so tense when somebody came into the house. I was never confident of how things looked. Struggling with clutter wore me out. Things are beginning to clear up for me now.

"I've started to group our belongings together (or I should say we all have been working on it) and to find a place to store them in containers. I've put labels on every container telling what is in it. The kids are looking at this and laughing at the labels, but I'll tell you something—it's working. I know where to get things and, what's more, where to put them back. Now when the children need something, I can tell them where it is instead of getting up to look for it with them. That alone is saving a lot of time and effort for me.

"Just knowing where things are makes me more relaxed. I still have more places and things to organize but now I know I can do it. I did not realize how much stress disorganization was causing me."

"Umm," I said, nodding. She had caught me with my mouth full. "And what about the kids? How's it going with them?" I perched my fork on the plate I was holding and it promptly fell into my lap. I hate it when I make a clutzy mess while I am talking about being neater.

Rosalie got me a damp cloth and talked while I wiped the juice from my skirt. "They seem to be some better," she said. "I've put our motto up in the kitchen, and we are trying to follow the rules you gave me for habit change: honoring the sanctity of family areas, following the camper's rule, and remembering the thirty second rule. You're right when you say if we could just apply these few rules consistently, the whole house would be easier to keep nice. The German grandmother's story in the e-mail was inspirational. I think I will read it to my family tonight at the table.

"But I can tell that this will not be enough. Our team is getting ready to play the organizing game. We've been practicing. We're getting the field ready. I've given pep talks. But we have yet to really get into the game and we sure aren't ready to be winners."

"Okay," I said. We need to talk about that all-important area of the whole plan and how the kids fit into it."

EIGHT

Managing the Kids

A mother's job is to train a dependent person to become an independent contributor.

Lydia wrote home from college thanking her mom for the training she had given her as a kid. She shared an apartment with four girls. One of them was way out in left field when it came to knowing how to take care of herself as an adult.

"She is so slow and she doesn't know how to do the ordinary things. We feel sorry for her because she just wasn't taught how to pull her weight. Now it's hard for her to learn. But I am not writing to complain about her. My real reason for writing is to say, Thank you! Thank you! Thank you! for all you did in training me in how to live."

Learning how to live organizationally is just one of the many skills we need to teach our children. It may not be number one on the list of priorities, but it takes on special importance because it's woven into almost every important area of life. In the case of Lydia's friend, lack of organizational skills interfered with her relationships with the other three girls and probably her schoolwork. Guess what her lack of knowledge will do in marriage, raising children, and even her future job. The importance of Mom being a good manager of housekeeping is supported by a recent study reported in the Associated Press. The conclusion of the twenty-five-year study covering 3,400 homes was that homes that were kept clean in an efficient way produced children who achieve more educationally and professionally than those raised in homes that were not efficiently managed. The article made a point to say that the important issue was not primarily how clean the house was but how efficiently it was managed. The lead researcher, Rachel Dunifon, suggested that children who grow up in an organized and clean home learn organizational skills from their parents that carry over into other areas of life.

Refocusing on Our Goals for Our Kids

Our goal as parents is not just to survive from one day to the next. It's not even to have a functional and pleasant house. Both of these are important. But, remember, our goal is not best expressed as the desire to eliminate clutter and messes from our house. It is not best expressed as the desire to keep our kids from being slobs when they have families of their own. That is looking at the negative aspect of the thing.

The positive aspect is this—our goal is to build beauty and order in our home and, more important, beautiful qualities in our children. As we have emphasized before, our primary goal is to raise children who will be capable and mature adults in all of the important areas of their lives. The house just happens to be one of the best playing fields on which to play this all-important game of raising our children to be truly mature adults.

Each day of harmonious working together, reaching goals that everyone can easily see and appreciate, builds character, a sense of purpose, a feeling of control, an understanding of responsibility, and a deep bond to others in the family. In short, we are producing children we can be proud of and, if they should think of it in that way, children who can be proud of the person they become as adults.

There are other arenas in the life of a child we can use to instill these positive qualities but none more constant or practical than working together with others in the home.

> Our primary goal is to raise children who will be capable and mature adults in all of the important areas of their lives.

Wherever you are on your way to achieving a goal, now is always the time to make improvements. It is never too late to start. If you have decided that your kids need help organizationally, step back, take a fresh look, and decide what your plan of action will be.

While living a full-blown Messie lifestyle, I raised my children well into their teen years. My youngest was a young teen when I started getting my act together organizationally. Did my family suffer? I think that in this regard they did. We did a good job in other areas, but they were not given training that they could use to their advantage in their present lives as adults.

Our kids do tend to survive our weaknesses, but they probably have to struggle harder than they would if they had received careful training.

Learning Styles

Consider the way your child learns best. Most of us have a one-size-fits-all approach. For most of us it is simple: You tell them what to do, show them to make sure they understand, write it down to reinforce it, and then—voilà! They do what you want. If it doesn't work, we go over it again, talking louder. That is the basic technique most parents use and it generally works pretty well. But it does not meet the needs of all children. Although children can learn through a variety of modalities, each child learns best if we understand his preferred mode of learning and make an effort to reach the child through that mode. If you don't know how your child learns best, try several different approaches and see which clicks. By doing this, you honor his individuality and teach him something that will be useful whenever the child is in a position of learning. You also make it easier on yourself. Why keep telling a child the steps to do when he may work best when shown or when the instructions are written or approached in some other way?

Here are a few suggestions for several learning modalities:

> *Visual.* Take pictures of areas of the rooms when they are in good shape, and put them on the chore chart. Provide a written checkoff list.
>
> *Auditory.* Talk about the jobs that need to be done. For younger children, make up a song to work by.
>
> *Kinesthetic.* Do the job with the child.
>
> *Group Learner.* Make plans together; emphasize teamwork.
>
> *Creative Learner.* Make a book with pictures of orderly rooms. Make a clay model of the room. Play a game or write a story involving the process of doing a job.

Some approaches we try will totally miss a child's learning mode. You may be trying to do a cooperative, group thing where you share ideas and plans, but you find you have a child who would rather you just tell him what to do so he can get on with it. Or you may have an in-depth discussion with a child, who in the process forgets what you wanted him to do, because he needs a checklist.

Billy was driving his sister crazy because he left the bathroom in disarray when he used it. Telling him, fussing, yelling did no good. His sister made a checklist (hang up towel, put soap in dish, put clothes in hamper, and so on), put it in a clear plastic cover, and taped it to the back of the door. Billy marked off each step with an erasable pen as he cleaned up. It worked! She was talking his language.

You don't have to be a trained educator to find how best to work with your child. Just be aware of the various learning modalities, be flexible, and try approaches other than the standard "tell and tell again louder" approach, and then watch for what "clicks" with your child.

Find Out What Matters to the Child

We have to be alert to what really reaches our child's psyche. Nobody changes unless he perceives it in a way that makes it important to him.

Neighbors were annoyed when school of theology students kept parking in the spaces in front of their homes. They tried NO PARKING signs. They had cars ticketed, then towed. They tried asking the students to park elsewhere. Nothing worked. The problem was solved when they put up a sign saying, "Thou shalt not park here." They had translated the parking issue into a spiritual one, and that made sense to the students.

Thousands of crows descended on a small community and stayed there causing lots of problems for the citizens. They tried everything they knew. They shot fireworks into the gathering, they used loud noises, they sent out dogs—you name it. Nothing worked until they hired a company who brought in trained hawks, an eagle, and tethered owls. Last count was just a little over four hundred crows. Nobody knows where the rest went. The crows responded when the citizens found out what mattered to the crows.

Rhonda kept getting in trouble in school. Her mom tried every punishment she knew to bring about change. Nothing got Rhonda's attention until Mom said that the next time the school called, she would go to school with Rhonda, sit in her classes with her, stand with her in the halls, and eat with her in the cafeteria. Rhonda changed!

Running into Roadblocks

When you have done your best to reach your child and are still running into barriers that just won't come down, you do well to move carefully. You may be dealing with a child who needs special consideration because he is battling undetected issues.

Keep your eye out for clues that the child may be distractible, depressed, have a hearing or vision problem, or a myriad of other interferences. Working together in the house is one of the best ways of discovering these problems.

Sometimes conditions that interfere with learning are the result of external problems and sometimes they are internal. Distractibility, for instance, may be a response to stress, may be attention deficit disorder, or may have some other cause. Sometimes just plain good parenting will solve the problem; sometimes it requires outside help.

It may be that problems you are experiencing in moving forward are the result of a poor relationship that has developed between you and your child. This is the time to sit down and start unraveling what might be the hindrance.

The Kid without a Clue about Organizing

Kids vary a lot in natural characteristics. Some characteristics are helpful and some cause trouble. A child who is color-blind is not going to do well in art class. A tone-deaf child will have trouble with music. Some kids are klutzes in sports. In the same way, some children seem to be born without organizational savvy. In our world, individuals don't have to participate in art, music, or sports all of their lives. But for his whole life, your child will have to use organizational skills because they are necessary in every area of life.

Difficulty with organization is called developmental disorganization and has many of the same characteristics as ADD. Developmental disorganization has not received the same attention as other learning disabilities, probably because it does not relate directly to academics. It is better thought of as a "living disability." Often parents blame the messiness they see in their developmentally disorganized children on laziness, procrastination, rebellion, or lack of caring.

As a parent, you may suspect that your child is developmentally disorganized if, compared to others his age, he has trouble estimating time; problems remembering sequences, such as the steps in telling a joke, or learning sequences, such as months or days of the week; trouble relating to space directional words, such as *above, below, right, left, after, before;* and difficulty following a sequence of directions. Some of these children may be accident-prone and clumsy.

The telltale signs to Mom are most likely to be a consistently messy room, failure to finish tasks, poor management of time and schedules, and frequent loss of possessions. In the child's schoolwork, the handwriting may be poor, poorly spaced, and "wandering," especially when he tries to make columns.

What no one sees on the outside, and the child is unable to evaluate for himself, is the inner turmoil that is taking place in the child's thinking. Ideas, words, learned material, and the like are not being successfully organized in the brain. There is a randomness in the child's thinking similar to the randomness seen in the child's room. Children with developmental disorganization fail to see patterns about the way life works and they don't recognize routines. Life is not logical for them. They don't sort or categorize in a meaningful way.

This leads to unexplained confusion on the child's part. These children don't realize that everyone doesn't process things with as much difficulty as they do. A smart child begins to feel dumb and a child with a sunny disposition begins to despair. Sometimes they are called underachievers by teachers and parents who see that they are smart but not producing. If we could see the internal difficulties they are overcoming we might want to call them overachievers.

Overcoming the Roadblocks

Once roadblocks are identified, parents can begin pursuing a way around them. For relational roadblocks, work on communication. When the problem is physical (such as vision or hearing), emotional (such as depression or stress), attention deficit disorder (which is not always accompanied by hyperactivity), or developmental disorganization, the pediatrician is probably the best place to start.

While receiving appropriate outside help, the parent can greatly improve many of these problems by setting up consistent systems, helping establish boundaries, and coaching the child in how to sort, categorize, and see patterns.

This may be done with toys, blocks, and other items in "games" like "Let's put all of the cars, all of the trucks, and all of the boats together in their own little area." A game of grouping socks, underwear, and sleepwear together in specific and consistent places is instructive to the child and accomplishes a household task at the same time.

Help the child set boundaries. Make certain rules such as, "Get out only five toys at a time. Put those away before you get out more." Or, "We clean up our belongings before dinner each night." By the way, although some make it a pattern to clean up before bedtime, it is probably best to clean up before dinner or shortly thereafter. If you wait until bedtime, avoid cleaning requirements that might cause tumult when you are trying to get the kids to relax.

People feel secure and gain comfort from predictability. The more information they have about what is happening and when, the less stress they experience. We do our children, who probably feel pretty powerless anyway, a big favor when we provide them with a life in which they know what is going on.

Make up written schedules for various key times during the day. Work with your child to carry them out. An example is this after-school schedule.

1. Snack
2. Homework (one hour)

3. Play outside (one hour)
4. TV (half hour)
5. Feed pets
6. Dinner

To tune children into how time passes, play time games such as, "See how much you can get done in the three minutes before this timer goes off." Another game is to guess how much time it takes to unload the dishwasher, make the bed, or any task while timing the activity.

Set Up for Success

Mom must set up the child's room so that the belongings flow easily in and out of their designated places. To do that she groups like things in baskets and clear boxes with large labels showing with words or pictures what is in the basket. She uses color coding where possible. She makes sure some toys are stored so the child is not overly stressed with having too much to manage. She consistently reminds the child that the systems are used so that things don't become disorganized and the child is unable to straighten them out.

In short, the disorganized child needs to have in place all of the organizational systems and props that any child might need. However, they need more consistency than is usually necessary. Of course, for many parents (who may themselves have a touch of the same tendency to disorder that the child does), the real problem is being consistent with their own schedules and following up on whether the child is keeping on schedule.

Bethany's daughter, Susan, was intelligent but "flaky" when it came to organizing. Bethany spoke to Susan's teachers and set up a notebook and book bag system of

Make It Easier for the Kids

Laundry—Teach them the steps of the washing process. When they are young, get a stool if they are too short to reach into the washer.

Breakfast—Keep bowls, spoons, cereal, or whatever you serve for breakfast on a shelf low enough for kids to reach by themselves.

Bed making—If the bed is hard to get to because it is pressed against the wall, tuck the spread between the mattress and box spring on the wall side and attach it to the mattress with safety pins or strong clips so the child has to pull up only one side in the morning. (Be careful with pins if your child is young.)

Putting away their things—Have a work area near where the family congregates. It can be a table or desk. In boxes or other containers nearby, locate work materials such as crayons, scissors, paper, pencils, and the like. For little ones, have a toy basket in every room for easy cleanup.

Color coding—Assign each child a color and use it in several areas. Buy two sets of towels in the assigned color for each child (one for use while the other is being washed). Wash towels once a week. When a towel is out of place, it is easy to see to whom it belongs. Glasses and cups can follow the same color pattern. Each person drinks from only his or her color all day. You may want to get socks with that color band on the top for easy identification.

Bathrooms—Put up hooks so kids can hang towels up easier than on towel racks.

organizing that the teachers reinforced in the classroom. At home, Bethany set up a schedule for her daughter. Now Susan, who was flirting with failure in several subjects because she could not get her organizational act together, is making *A*'s. Bethany is bewildered as to why her daughter can't do this herself but she is heartened that the changes they have made work for her. And Susan is much happier now that she can perform at her ability level.

Ensuring a Successful Plan

There are hundreds of tips, really useful tips, for getting children to cooperate in doing housework. Trying to put too many tips into practice, especially at one time, will only overwhelm both you and your children.

The success you are looking for comes from keeping your vision, making a simple but powerful managerial plan, and applying that consistently to your family. Here is a summary of the plan:

1. Show and tell your family how to do each job that is their responsibility.
2. Make a step-by-step procedure using pictures or written steps.
3. Work with them until they can do the job alone.
4. Watch them do it until you are sure they can do it alone.
5. Leave written or picture reminders so they will be very clear about your expectations.
6. Inspect and evaluate their work when they do it alone.

This plan covers most of the learning modes. If your child has a specific learning mode not included here, develop your plan with your child's need in mind.

Games and Fun Activities

Little children love rhyming. Poetry is easier to remember than prose and more fun! Anke Volke in

Germany uses little poems to remind her children what to do. This comes naturally to her, and couplets such as this, in German of course, spring to her lips easily:

> The room gets the blues
> When you leave out your shoes.

Another one might be the American favorite:

> Boys who are neat,
> Lift the seat.
> When they are through,
> They put it down too.

Or its companion verse dealing with basic bathroom skills:

> If you sprinkle
> When you tinkle,
> Please be sure
> To wipe the floor.

If a mom can think of these easily and repeat a few of the important ones over and over when the child is very young, soon the child will hear a little voice spouting poetry in his head as he goes about the business of living.

Time It: Use a stop watch to time how long your child takes to clean up. Then next time, see if he or she cleans faster.

Race the Bell: Set an alarm for a reasonable time and see if your child can beat the bell.

Bell Break: Set up an alarm and when it sounds, take a clean-up break. If your child is more than half done when the buzzer sounds, offer an award or a big hug and praise.

To Bed, to Bed: Tell your child that clean-up means bedtime for toys and animals. Let your child kiss animals and dolls goodnight and gently place them in their places (beds). Play lullaby music during this activity.

Picture Perfect: When the room is clean take a photo. You might want to have it made into a poster. Hang it in the room. Then at clean-up, have your child check the picture to see where things belong. See if the child can again get the room picture perfect.

Draw Cleaning Lots: Write down each of the cleaning jobs that need to be done. Let your child draw one slip out at a time and do that job. Take a break before drawing the next job. Continue until all the work is done. Or let your child draw one job each day.

A Chronic Mistake

A chronic mistake made by Manager-moms is to let things go too far without intervening and then coming down too strongly on the offender. In relation to the house, the Manager-mom can let the condition of the child's room deteriorate to such a degree that it would bring a professional organizer to her knees with despair. Periodically this type of mom reaches her limit. To get the mess cleaned up, she begins threatening, punishing, and browbeating the child she has consistently allowed to live in chaos.

In contrast, successful Manager-moms keep on top of the situation on a day-to-day basis, nipping the rising clutter in the bud by training, encouraging, and supervising before it mushrooms into a monumental mess.

Living Skills and Self-Esteem

One source of self-esteem comes from testing one's abilities and succeeding. Self-reliance and independence bring appropriate self-confidence. When, by hard work and practice, children accomplish a task that they thought was beyond them, they have reason to be happy about that accomplishment and what it means about their skills. Usually the struggle and accomplishment are more important than the task itself.

Living skills that make the child more and more able to take care of himself and contribute to the family team as a whole are probably the best arena at our disposal for developing a truly strong inner person.

What Words to Use

When the child is just beginning and the work turns out poorly, the parent may wish to ignore the problems if the beginner did his best. Instead, compliment the effort with a statement that does not address how well the job is done, something like, "Your bed's made already. I like that." Or, "I think you can probably do a little better with those wrinkles underneath. I'll show you how tomorrow." Or, "Is there any part of this you think could be improved?" Don't redo a beginner's work. The next morning, work with the child to improve it as part of your ongoing training.

Accepting poor work as okay when a child has not done his best signals to the child that you don't expect much of him. In his mind that translates into *I'm not worth much, I guess.* Or *Others have to work to succeed. I guess I don't.*

It's probably not necessary to mention that labeling and name-calling belittles and discourages a child.

Friendly Daily Reminders

I learned the idea of using reminder statements written on cards from the manager of a restaurant in a large hotel chain. He reads one daily and so should we. Here are some of the ones I've used:

> In our family, we clear the table and clean the kitchen together.
>
> In our family, we hang up the towels neatly after bathing.
>
> In our family, we put what we need to take to school or work the next day by the front door the night before.
>
> In our family, we don't drop our things when we come in the door. We put them where they belong.
>
> In our family, we put dirty clothes into the hamper as soon as we take them off.
>
> In our family, we put things back where they belong as soon as we finish with them.
>
> In our family, we make our beds before we leave our room in the morning.
>
> In our family, we put dirty dishes in the dishwasher not in the sink.
>
> In our family, we take responsibility for completing the chores assigned to us.
>
> In our family, we don't complain about our responsibilities.

Three Levels of Praise

- Focus on evaluating the work not the child. If the room is nice and clean before you leave for school, a statement such as, "Your room looks nice this morning," may be enough.
- Focus on the child's part. Occasionally mentioning the child's part in the work is appropriate. Add, "You did a good job."
- Speak of the child's qualities. Very occasionally make a personal evaluation such as, "You are a very good cleaner!" And then only when it is really warranted.

A ricochet compliment works well on occasion. Brag on a child's accomplishment to someone else in his hearing: "Brad has been getting ready for school five minutes early lately. I think it is because he's gotten his room so well organized."

If someone mentions something good about your child to you, ask him or her to tell the child. Praise is special coming from a disinterested source.

Praise works because it makes the child feel good. He or she will want to return to behaviors that lead to those good feelings. Remember, praise must be used judiciously for it to retain its value.

Eventually, the child will begin to have a built-in sense of satisfaction when he or she does well according to his or her own standards. Then we're getting somewhere!

In our family, we always flush the toilet immediately after using it.

In our family, we put away toys, games, tools, and stuff immediately after finishing with them.

In our family, we don't leave things out just because we plan to get back to the project later.

In our family, we wash, dry, fold, and put away our clothes as one continuous job.

In our family, we make sure all trash goes into the trash basket.

In our family, we value each other and the contribution each makes.

In our family, we keep our closets and drawers neat.

In our family, we use the team concept. Each person does his or her part to support all.

In our family, we are willing to help others where necessary because we are a team.

In our family, we don't make messes or create work for others.

In our family, we don't boss others. We focus on our own responsibilities.

In our family, we speak kindly to each other.

In our family, we try to think ahead to solve problems before they happen.

In our family, we pay attention to maintaining beauty.

In our family, we push our chairs up to the table when we get up from it.

In our family, we use one bath towel for a week.

In our family, we change our bedsheets every two weeks.

In our family, we strive to complete projects and clean up expeditiously.

In our family, the person who uses the last sheet of toilet paper puts a new roll on the roller.

In our family, we make a list on the white board of what we need from the store.

In our family, we move the garbage cans out of sight after they are emptied at the curb.

You may wish to use these reminders or write thirty or thirty-one for yourself to cover a month. If the habit of reading the reminders is well established by then, start the cycle again. Or perhaps you will want to pick a few important reminders and recycle them regularly during the month. If you decide to stop doing this regularly with your children or the habit drifts away, return to it every once in a while. You can play catch-up by giving each person a reminder at a meal so several are read. Refer to the reminders as you work together around the house.

Take care not to use a reminder as the text of a long sermon or to browbeat your kids with it. Hit them lightly (the topics, not the kids) and move on, or your family may begin to think of the reminders as nuisances, rather than important parts of a larger and important goal. Sometimes a reminder may be the springboard for a compliment when you say, "I think we have been doing well on that one," and then point out some specific way that is true.

At the risk of being both redundant and repetitive, I want to encourage you to use reminders regularly but don't discuss them at any length. Like salt, a little is good but too much ruins the whole dish.

Copping a 'Tude

I think more and more that at some level everybody, myself included, wants to be coddled and taken care of. The desire to be independent and self-sufficient fights with the urge to be dependent. As we mature, the independent part overpowers the dependent part. But that fight doesn't happen quietly.

When you tell your kids to straighten their rooms or set the table, they may rebel. They may whine, maybe stomp a foot, dawdle, or do whatever it takes to stay helpless. They display an angry attitude because they are resisting independence.

Change is always scary. To shift from the security of being taken care of by a strong and wise adult to being cared for by an inexperienced child—oneself—is definitely risky. In some cases, kids resist independence because they fear the unknown of growing up.

The Manager-mom who is training her children needs to do so with a great deal of encouragement. If we as adults believe that our child can make it, can do a good job of learning the skills necessary to become a competent adult who can not only take care of himself or herself but others as well, we will communicate that to him or her in numerous ways both conscious and unconscious.

Sometimes they will say, "I can't" about doing a job you believe they are capable of doing. This is always a good opportunity to say, "Apparently I have more confidence in you than you have in yourself. I believe you can. I'm older and wiser than you are." It may be appropriate to add, "I'll help you get started," as you start to work and, if necessary, evaluate and train further.

It may be that this little talk will do little or no good in overcoming resistance at this particular point and you may need to go to consequences. But the fact that you have expressed confidence in your child and continue to do so when this happens again will start to sink in and be beneficial to him or her in the long run.

As we are proactive in understanding our children's individual needs and setting out to meet them, our kids will have the confidence to try without copping a 'tude at every turn.

I suggest you read *Solid Answers* by Dr. James Dobson (Wheaton: Tyndale House, 1997). In this 576-page book, Dr. Dobson answers from a Christian perspective tough questions facing today's families on this topic. It includes a chapter on attention deficit disorder in children and a lot of information about discipline, covering younger children and teens.

Aim for Excellence, Not Perfection

We are not expecting perfection, but we do our children a favor when we instill in them an attitude of excellence. We want them to do their best in a way consistent with the circumstances. Housework is an area where "good enough" often is just fine. But the overall effect of what we do has got to meet our goal.

In other words, when our child makes his bed, the covers may not be totally flat, but the room looks good. The main dish of the dinner made by our teen may be a store-bought family-size entrée. He may have served canned vegetables and a prewashed bagged salad, but the table looks good, the family eats happily, and you all work as a team to clear the table and clean the kitchen. This has the ring of excellence.

The Teen's Room, the Seat of the Soul

Special consideration needs to be given to the room of teenagers. Children's rooms have long been much more than a place to sleep and dress. It is where they entertain themselves and do their homework. It may be where friends gather and where they work on the computer. A teenager's room expresses individuality and creativity.

Some teens may lose interest in their rooms at a certain point when outside interests take over. Or sometimes an ordinarily neat teen may decide to try on a cluttered lifestyle to see how he likes it. Usually the teen will find the neater way is much easier to live with. A common occurrence is for teens to begin to practice adult homemaking skills, using their rooms to experiment with personal style.

Your teen may plaster his walls with pictures of his celebrity idol of the moment or of his friends. He may go for a theme room showcasing his hobby or a special interest. Supporting decorating that makes your child proud will encourage him to keep it nice. Your house and your teen's room can be a magnet that will lure friends over. Having your child love to be home and getting to know his all-important friends are important reasons for having an inviting house.

In the book *The Second Family*, Dr. Ron Taffel recounts how the parents of seventh-grader Kirk set out to make their house a kid-friendly place for Kirk's six or eight best buddies. As a sort of rite of passage, they helped Kirk decorate and organize his room with the express purpose of accommodating friends. They stocked up on kid food, much of which, but not all, was healthy.

They had several rules that they personally made clear to Kirk's friends. They specifically didn't put Kirk in the position of having to monitor his friends' behavior. One rule was each friend had to call his folks as soon as he came in as the price of admission. Each also had to take off shoes at the door on muddy days, wrap and put food back when finished eating, and keep the counter clean. No smoking was allowed.

Kirk's folks made his friends feel welcome by being friendly and providing a place for them to feel comfortable. But they made sure by making and enforcing the rules that everybody knew the adults were in charge. There was a casual atmosphere. Kids would wander out of Kirk's room to banter with his parents, and the room was definitely not off-limits to the adults who popped in now and again to chitchat.

A word of warning may be in order when planning a teen's room. Some teens may begin cocooning in their rooms if they have television, phone, computer, CD player, their own bathroom, and other supports that enable them to stay in their room in a sort of semi-apartment situation. Although children need to have a place where they can find moments of solitude, it is important to keep them rubbing elbows with fellow team members of the family on a regular basis.

Bonding

None of these ideas will work without bonding. Bonding is the glue that holds it all together. If what you try to put into practice is not slathered heavily with a strong bond with your kids, your plan will fall apart. If the third, smart little pig had built his brick house perfectly and failed to use mortar, his house too would have fallen apart. You must have the mortar of a strong personal relationship with those you lead.

Fortunately many of the ideas already presented will strengthen the bonds we have with our kids. When we take their individual learning styles into consideration, we bond. As we teach them how to live and support them in their maturing, we bond. When we disagree, tangle, and come out on the other side with some satisfactory understanding, we bond. Asserting your dominance and leadership appropriately establishes a strong bond with your child. Daily living offers many natural ways to bond.

Our connection with our children is not generally supported by the society in which we live. There is not room in this book to explain how parental authority is undermined by various forces. One of these forces is the pace of living that pulls us away from one another in the family to go to work, classes, social opportunities outside the family, and the like. We hardly have time together. Consider the following:

- Among children ages eight to twelve, almost one-third say they do not spend enough time with their fathers.

- Twenty percent of sixth through twelfth graders say they have not had a good conversation with at least one of their parents in more than a month, although there are 43,200 minutes in a month.

- Parents today spend roughly 40 percent less time (or ten to twelve hours per week) with their children than did parents a generation ago.

It is clear that we must take care to maintain a strong relationship with our children. Counselors report that younger children are generally sad about their lack of interaction and time with parents. If it continues, older children tend to become belligerent. Because they can be more independent, teens tend to seek fulfillment outside the home by bonding with peers as a substitute for what parental relationships may lack.

To establish a close relationship, we must seek to know, really know, our kids. We must listen to them and try to understand their needs, but that doesn't mean we forget our expectations of them. We must not be so empathetic that we let them do whatever they want, nor should we be so authoritarian, we fail to consider their interests. We want them to feel both heard and held. Even if we don't understand or even fully approve of their interests, we can be curious about and try to appreciate what interests them. I have spent recent times discussing Pokemon characters with an eight year old (made no sense to me at all), fishing with an eleven year old, and rolling a ball with a two year old. None of these are of any personal interest to me (well, the fishing maybe) but I have a higher priority than entertaining myself. There are important young lives growing in the garden of my influence that must be tended.

Rules without relationship lead to rebellion.

It will never be easy to hit it exactly right—the right balance of showing we care while providing strong leadership. We can, however, strive to do our best. Living with children, especially teens, is a complex dance. In that dance, we work to really relate to our kids. It is only when they feel understood and cared about that they are open to leadership.

The best place to practice that dance is in our own homes. Sure, we'll step on toes, we'll get out of sync with the music, sometimes we'll dance to different tunes. But we'll communicate along the way and teach life skills there, we'll be interested in uninteresting things, we'll make home a place where we take our togetherness seriously, we'll establish areas where all are refreshed as individuals, and we will lure our kids' friends in by having a comfortable environment that works right. In short, we'll make a really good home.

That's what all of this Visionary-mom and Manager-mom stuff is all about. It's about how you can become the most powerful force possible in accomplishing the most important goal in your life. Just being a more efficient and energetic Worker-mom will not come close to touching that high goal.

Rosalie's Response

Rosalie laughed a hearty laugh when we met to discuss goals for kids in caring for the home. "You have really laid it on thick this time," she said, shaking her head and smiling as she sipped her sweet, hot cortadito. Cortadito means "little cut" in Spanish because the espresso is cut with less milk than cafe con leche. It's a favorite in Miami among Hispanics and Anglos alike. It occurred to me that Rosalie might be Hispanic in background. Who can tell anymore? "An excellent choice, madam," said the server behind the counter who wore the name tag "Angel," a common Hispanic name.

We had met at the local coffee emporium. It was midmorning. The hot sun was streaming through the plateglass windows as we sat in two dark purple easy chairs with a small table between us. Late spring was giving way to summer. I wondered how Rosalie downed her steaming drink in the heat.

Trying to keep cool, I had gotten an iced caramel mocha decaf made with no-fat milk and artificial sweetener. "Totally neutered," the guy who made it murmured. I wish there had also been some way to neutralize the calories in the sweet caramel that made it so good. I pulled the cool mixture up the straw and looked at Rosalie.

"Remember, the focus is not the house," I said, obviously repeating myself. "You are moving out of the Worker mentality into the Manager-mom mentality. Do what you have to do to get the housework done while you are getting the team in place. Use paper plates, cooking shortcuts, or whatever. But focus on training the family to work as a team and each team member to be able to play his or her position.

"All the while, remember that your goal goes way beyond the house. There are a lot of reasons the house is important but the main one is that it is the place your family learns to function to its fullest potential. You want to make a place where your kids feel safe and comfortable, a place where they want to be.

"Only when they know you love them wisely but won't let them get away with things will you be in a position to influence them in all areas of their lives.

"I've been on the Internet myself and found some interesting postings," I said, trying to scoop up with my straw some of the caramel that had solidified on the ice. "There are a lot of women working to achieve the same goals you are. We'll need to look at the practicalities of some of these ideas we have been covering and what others have to say about how they apply them."

NINE

Management Ideas Meet Reality

I cleaned my house yesterday. Sure wish you could have seen it.

Do you remember the story told by the owner of the Texas hunting dog? He learned that what he thought he was doing right wasn't working with his dog. His words were, "I was just uneducated about how to apply what I had learned from books. After talking to my friend, I did three things different. I made my directions to the dog much clearer. I was consistent in how I gave them. And I followed up to make sure they were followed. When I corrected those things, the dog got much better."

You have been making plans for managing your family. For it to work, you have got to do the same three things:

- Make your directions very, very clear by writing, using pictures, showing, making placards, or whatever it takes to make sure you are understood.

- Be very, very consistent in your expectations, your directions, and your follow-up.

- Always follow up to be sure that the project has been done (children will do what you inspect, not what you expect), and stick with it until it is actually completed.

Advice from Mothers

Let's look at various ways other moms have put these ideas into practice.

How to Manage the Toys

Jenny, a young mother who decided to begin managing her house, asked for help with toys from other struggling moms who had already gone down that road.

One mom's reply to Jenny shows how she uses her newly emerging managerial skills. Perhaps you will catch some of her enthusiasm as you read.

You must BOX UP all the toys, leaving out only two favorites for each child. I know it sounds drastic, but you will get IMMEDIATE results with this—I know!! I was going crazy with endless toy clutter—all the game pieces were mixed up, half scattered all over upstairs and half scattered downstairs. I finally declared marshall law and put all their toys in large boxes and put them away! Then they were expected to pick up and take care of the ones they had. Once they showed they could be responsible, they could have another toy, or they could trade an old toy for a new one. I did this last year—the kids have not missed the boxed-up toys and they have been very good about keeping what they have picked up. They didn't like feeling overwhelmed either. When they get bored, they ask to "trade" and we do.

Another mom wrote of her approach as follows:

Jenny,
Whatever mess my kids make, they are made responsible to clean. "You mess it, you clean it" is a constant saying in my home. Whenever they whine or complain about doing it, I say, "If you don't like cleaning up messes, what makes you think that I like cleaning them? Do you think it's fair if I made you clean up all the messes Mommy, Daddy, sister, and baby make? If it's not fair to expect that from you, is it fair to expect that from Mommy?"

As far as the juice spilling goes—get those sipper cups!! They are a godsend! My kids were not allowed outside of the kitchen without a sipper cup. My son is eight and doesn't need one, but he still will use one occasionally "so his sister won't knock it over." I used to let him take drinks in his room, but he never brought the cups back, so I told him that he lost the privilege and couldn't have it back unless he shows he can be responsible with returning the cups. I explained that privileges are EARNED, and when he's old enough to handle the responsibility, then he can have the privilege back. So far, so good.

My kids also know that they do not eat in the living room or on the couch. They of course still bring food in and I immediately send them back to the dining room. I give them appropriate information: "Couches are for SITTING ON—tables are for EATING ON. You know the rules." And they go back in the dining room.

I know it's hard to be firm (not mean!) with kids constantly, but they really do like having rules (and their future spouses will thank you).

Dear Jenny,
You wrote: "I have tried to enforce no eating outside of the kitchen/DR/outside deck like someone suggested, and have limited eating in my car to an occasional apple."
What were the results of this? Were you challenged? My kids challenged me because my rules were never consistent. Once I made them consistent, they stopped challenging and knew what was expected. If you like the results of not scrubbing up food all over the house, then you're on the right track. Keep enforcing those rules!

Little by Little Does the Trick

Longtime chronic problems don't go away overnight. Big, wonderful objectives are not achieved quickly. Your best bet is to proceed slowly but surely down the road you have chosen. Take a few small steps, test to see how it works with your child before you go on, and cement what works into your habits. Be very, very consistent with whatever few rules or changes you make. Then take another small step. Consistently follow the rules yourself.

Don't overload yourself with changes. No matter how good the ideas are, you won't follow through with them if you make too many changes too quickly. While the human spirit is not set in cement, it does become rather hardened around old habits, no matter how bad they are, and finds it hard to move to new habits, no matter how good.

In her post to the group, Amber tells us how changing habits worked for her.

I was just going over my checklist for today, and realized that I've really come a long way since joining you all!

I actually have a daily maintenance program in place! It took me a long time to internalize the advice of many of you to "find out what's important to you, pick 2 or 3 things to start with, and then just do them every day." I finally picked 3 things that are essential for me to feel in control of the house—dishes, scooping the cat box, and taking out the trash. I have managed all week to pay attention to these 3 areas every day. Just being able to consistently remember they exist, much less deal with them daily, is a big triumph for me.

I've also added one more thing, the "10-minute tidy." On the show "The Big Comfy Couch" (you can tell I have a little one!) the main character does a "10-second tidy" where she runs around in fast-forward for 10 seconds and just picks up and puts away all the toys she's dumped all over the floor and the couch during the rest of the episode. It was helpful with my son when he was little— we'd set a timer, and clean his room like crazy for 5 minutes. But somehow we stopped using it, and I've only this week remembered how effective it was. I set my timer for 10 minutes, and then pick a different area of the apartment each day to declutter. The object is to clear off all horizontal surfaces and "black hole areas" (like the big chair in the living room) that attract random clutter. I'm not allowed to move furniture—just pick up stuff and put it back in the room it belongs in. Even if it doesn't have a home, it still goes back in that room so that when I declutter that room, everything that belongs in it is there somewhere.

I also scheduled 2 longer decluttering sessions during the week—one on Wednesdays (early release day at my son's school) and one on Saturdays (my stay-at-home day right now). On Wednesdays I only have an hour to declutter, so I focus on one room. On Saturdays, I have 2 hours, so 2 rooms get my attention. I've written out a schedule of which rooms get attention on which days, and I don't feel so pressured to pay attention to "critical mass" rooms instead of high-payoff areas like the living room, because I know every room will get attention at least once a week. My living room looks a lot better, and my kitchen, dining room and bath are a lot less frightening.

I gave myself permission occasionally to go off-schedule and do one "diddle job" that either makes me feel good or serves a specific immediate need. Like sorting my jewelry.

Encouraging Good Behavior

There are two categories of changing behavior. We want both to stop bad behavior and to start good behavior. In addition to stopping unacceptable behavior, like dropping toys and clothes in the living room, we want the kids to begin doing activities like joining with the family to clean the kitchen each evening or doing their chores.

Training children to keep a neat room and to help the family with chores comes under the category of encouraging good behavior. Thomas Phelin says in his book *1–2–3 Magic: Effective Discipline for Children 2–12* that "cleaning bedrooms may be the chief cause of parent-child quarrels among all start-behavior problems." One way to encourage good behavior is pretty simple—you notice and reward it.

First, determine the good behavior you want to encourage. In the case of neatness, you communicate what behavior you want from the child. Then you appropriately and consistently reward it. There are various ways of doing that. A few samples are suggested but there are many more.

- *Straightforward schedule approach.* A simple schedule is made and each person is expected to follow the schedule. One family does this by having an outdoor list and an indoor list. The two boys of the family must do their chores after school before they can go out to play. Each week they alternate the lists. Because it is simple, has variety, and is easy to maintain, this method works well and has a longer life span than most. They can go out to play when finished.

- *Lottery approach.* Chores are written on slips of paper or Popsicle sticks, which are put into a cup. After dinner each person chooses one and does the chore he or she chooses. The family members pick up a cookie, piece of candy, or some small favor when they return their Popsicle stick to the cup.

- *Teamwork approach.* The family takes a period of time (perhaps using a timer) and does jobs that were divided up beforehand. Often jobs are done by a two-person team. Sometimes the whole family works as a group. The family may meet back together for popcorn, dessert, or a video. Nobody can eat until everybody has finished his or her job.

- *Chore chart.* The mom writes four or five chores on a piece of paper, checks off the chores on the chart each day as they are done, and rewards the good job in some predetermined way. Various types of chore charts can be found in appendix 5.

- *Contract.* Sometimes if there is one specific behavior that needs improving, the parents and child write out a contract that spells out the exact behavior, the reward for doing that behavior, and consequence for not doing it. Each contract has a time limit. Parents and child sign the contract. (See appendix for a contract form.)

All of these approaches tend to have a short life span. They are used to get the family started, to help the manager get her ideas organized, and to bring a family whose commitment is wandering back in focus.

To avoid boredom while using these approaches, switch around from time to time. When you set one up, you may plan to use it for only a month or so. Terminate an approach before it grinds to a halt from lack of attention. You may wish to take a break from a reward system involving treats and privileges for a while and use a more informal approach of reminders and verbal appreciation. You may simply say, "Your room looks nice, Jimmy." The old, tried-and-true "Before you can, you must . . ." approach, as in "Before you can go out, you must pick up your toys," is always useful. Be careful not to drift away from the reward concept. It is easy just to drop it because "they should do it anyway." Rewards are a must.

Once you get your own ideas organized about what you want to do, make the house ready for orderly living, train the children for their part, and get a routine going, you won't need to use any of these heavy-duty ideas. The real secret of having an orderly house is based on an approach that integrates training, motivation, consequences, and personal family commitment so seamlessly that someone from the outside looking in will think you just got lucky and were blessed with naturally orderly kids. Only you will know how it all came about.

It's like flying a plane. Getting it off the ground takes a lot of know-how. After that you can fly without much effort and even put it on autopilot for a while. I caution you, though, the Manager-mom needs to keep her eye on the process at all times. The household plane will never fly totally without supervision. Left to itself, it will likely crash rather quickly.

Consequences

Your children will challenge you for a number of reasons. They want to see if you are going to be consistent this time (perhaps, unlike past times). They will do it because they don't want to change their comfortable old habits. They will challenge to see whether you can maintain your control and for many other reasons. In a recent survey by *Ladies Home Journal,* 17 percent of the moms who responded said that disciplining their children was the part of motherhood they disliked most. We would all love to avoid discipline and, in truth, by managing your house well you can avoid much discipline that was needed previously. Being alert to the child's characteristics and wise mothering head off some problems.

While nobody really likes disciplining, it comes with the package called motherhood and can't be totally avoided. Since that is so, you need to be well prepared for what to do when the challenge comes. All discipline should be exercised with the goal in mind of changing the child's behavior and should be approached with a clear head and warm heart. Obviously our chief goal is the child's good. The secondary goal is the house.

There are several kinds of consequences you can use. All may be appropriate at one time or another. Lynn Clark breaks down mild punishment into five types in his excellent book *SOS! Help for Parents: A Practical Guide for Handling Common Everyday Behavior Problems.*

Time-out

Time-out is very effective for most children ages two to twelve. Isolating the child for unacceptable, usually explosive, behavior is a method often used by parents because it is gentle and usually does the job. If overused or used carelessly, however, it loses its effectiveness. For example, the child who stamps her foot and says no to picking up her toys goes to a time-out spot to be bored, think about changing her behavior, and calm down. After a discussion about picking up toys, she picks them up.

Scolding and Disapproval

Scolding and disapproval are usually moderately effective. Stating displeasure with the child's behavior should be done without rancor and at the child's eye level. For example, you could say, "I was very disappointed when I came home this afternoon and saw the mess you made in the living room. I expected better behavior than that from you. That's not the way we do things in our family." You may want to go on to ask, "When I come home tomorrow, can I count on you to have the living room looking nice?" Wanting to please mom is a very strong motivator for most children.

Natural Consequences

Simply allowing natural consequences to follow behavior is sometimes effective. The behavior carries its own punishment. Examples are clothes left unwashed because they were not put in the hamper or losing a left-out baseball mitt because the dog carried it away.

One mom started serving the food to her family on the surface of the table itself because the child whose job it was to set the table was still watching television. When the other children saw what was happening, they made sure the slow one got busy and did her work pronto. Do you think she was as likely to procrastinate the next time? Or ever again? Do you think this funny story probably went into the family archives and was told around tables into the next generation? That was one creative natural consequence!

Logical Consequences

Allowing the logical consequences of behavior can be effective, beginning at age three. The consequence relates logically to the misbehavior. For example, Mom takes away toys that are not replaced on the shelf. (They go to a "jail" box way up high because they broke the law or are given away to someone who will take care of them.)

Behavior Penalty

Though behavior penalties are not logically related to the misbehavior, they can be effective, beginning at age five. For example, the child can't listen to her stereo after school because she forgot to feed the dog that morning. Slapping the hand that throws food on the floor is another example of a behavior penalty.

Conscience Approach

As the children grow older and their sensitivity matures, you may wish to take the approach author and psychologist Kevin Leman used with his daughters after he asked them to clean up dog poop in the yard. When they didn't do it, he went out and started the distasteful task himself. Shortly, his daughters joined him, their consciences tweaked by his action. Of course, this assumes you have sensitive children. It might become ineffective if used too often. It won't work with those who might be glad that "poor old dad" got taken advantage of again. You have got to know your kids.

Flexible Approaches

Don't drop the whole idea of managing if you try an approach that works for a while and then begins to falter. The kids may become immune to it. More than likely, you will get tired of it and start being inconsistent. Stop, evaluate what is occurring, and make changes that will keep you on track. Tweak your system; keep improving it.

Be consistent with your expectations yet flexible with your approaches. Remember, nothing works forever with children—or adults for that matter. You need to be creative in your management skills until you find what works for both you and your kids.

Rosalie's Response

"Well, when we started getting so practical, I moved ahead with my family. First, I talked to Ben about what you and I have been talking about and he was all for it. He has always felt that as a leader of the church, he should set a good example. But we sure weren't setting much of an example in the upkeep of our home.

"I talked to each of the kids individually, not in a serious face-to-face way, but just as we were together casually. Then I waited a few days for the idea to sink in. We had already made some changes, so they sort of knew what I was aiming at. Of course, the motto and signs help a lot too.

"We had a family meeting and everybody agreed to cooperate with the plans I was putting in place. As long as we were just talking about it, the kids were fine with it. But when they actually had to make behavior changes, I began to get flak.

"I chose two problem areas to begin with—the bathroom and cleaning up after dinner. Here's what I did about the bathroom. I chose two towels for each person and put their names on them with a permanent marker. When one is in use, the other is being washed. I did this because some of them would dump the towels in the hamper to keep from hanging them up. Sometimes they just left them on the floor. Now each person has only one towel a week that he or she must hang up in a certain spot. Each person has his or her own color of towel and matching wash cloth. The color is a dead giveaway if somebody's towel is out of place. I think we may need to get another towel or two for Beth to use shampooing her hair.

"I got each child a bucket the same color as the towels. I put their names on the buckets. Each person keeps his or her toiletries, which I also marked with names, in the bucket and takes it to his or her bedroom when it is not in use in the bathroom. The bathroom used to be a wreck with all their things spread around. Now it's clear all the time. Wow! What a difference!

"If anybody leaves something in the bathroom that shouldn't be there, I take it. To get it back, they have to do a job for me, since I had to do a pickup job for them.

"As for the kitchen, everyone has an after-dinner cleanup job. Suffice it to say, we all leave the kitchen at the same time and it looks wonderful when we do. I used to be there long after everybody else had gone."

She sat back, looking happy and proud of what her family had achieved. "They didn't like it, but it is fair and they know it. I'm going to make sure these new habits get cemented before I introduce any more. But I can tell you that just these two things have made a big difference."

"I suspect the biggest difference is that you have really begun to discover the power of your managerial skills," I said.

"Umm, you may be right," she said, looking away and smiling a little.

"It's time you made a field trip to the house of Lenore, a friend of mine. I've learned a lot from her. Let me set it up for you, and we'll meet back together after your visit so you can tell me about your experience."

Part 3

A New View of Housekeeping

TEN

The Field Trip

There is a color, a tone, a resonance in the well ordered
life which is unknown in the life of disorder.

Sandra Felton

Rosalie and I had made a dinner appointment at a local
open-air seafood restaurant popular on Key Largo,
south of Miami. Set on Florida Bay, it overlooks small
islands set in an expanse of blue. Ben was holding down
the fort taking care of the children at home so we
wouldn't have to rush. We had made it a point to arrive
early before the crowd to get a table outside on the large
dock so we would be positioned to catch the sunset. On
the beach beside the dock, in a stand of palms, a native
of the Bahamas played island songs on steel drums.
Rosalie seemed excited to begin her story. I sensed it
was an important night for both of us. And indeed it
was.

In this idyllic setting Rosalie told me about her visit
with Lenore.

The House

"I arrived at Lenore's house about ten o'clock in the morning," she began. "Lenore had told me we would have a lot to talk about. I felt like I had made a business appointment. In a way it was. But it was not like any business appointment I had ever had."

I munched on grilled redfish, slaw, and baked potato as she described what she had seen. She told me that Lenore's house looked different from the houses around it. The lawn was green and manicured. Impatiens bloomed in the flower bed across the front of her house. Lenore had begonias in a pot on the front porch.

The front of the house had a brick porch. Her house was beige, trimmed in blue. It is a common color scheme in southern areas like Georgia but unusual in the tropical atmosphere of southern Florida.

Rosalie described the house as beautiful inside with a country flavor that's also a little unusual in Miami. Lenore had made lovely white slipcovers with dark blue welts for her living room furniture. An oriental rug with a rose background picked up the blue and beige in the rest of the room and tied in with other rose accents. Blue willow vases and pottery complemented the decor.

As Lenore gave Rosalie a tour of the house, she told her she had gotten a lot of things at yard sales and by frequenting the Salvation Army store on Saturday morning when the truck came in with fresh deliveries. She seemed delighted with the whole challenge of making a lovely home by putting together pieces she collected from unlikely sources. "It's like going on a treasure hunt!" she said.

The children's rooms were of special interest to Rosalie. Lenore's daughter's room was small, but it had a lovely decor with a quilt on the bed and a comforter folded at the foot. She had lots of pillows at the head of the bed. Her daughter has several hobbies and interests, so the room was chockfull of things teens like to have around them. But she had taken time and effort to make sure they were displayed neatly. Lenore said it got pretty untidy during the week sometimes but was always cleaned up by Saturday night.

Her son's room was simpler and easier to keep neat. A few things were out. Lenore said that he knows they need to be put away before friends can come over or before he can go out to anybody's house. (Note how she has built in rewards naturally.) It's interesting, she said, that her daughter has drifted away from making her bed every day as she taught her, but her son does it pretty faithfully. Lenore said she is flexible on some things but makes sure some lines are never crossed.

Lenore's Plan

Rosalie really wanted to know exactly how Lenore got the house looking so good and how she kept it that way. "That was the really important part to me," said Rosalie. "And she didn't disappoint me!"

She stopped to eat some of her fish. Dipping a french fry into catsup, she continued.

"I got right to the point," Rosalie continued. "I told her I felt like I was just a beginner and asked her if she had always been so neat and organized. We sat with a glass of coke in her living room and she explained how she had developed her family plan for organizing.

"She said that when she first got married their first apartment was pretty messy. She didn't seem to be able to keep house like her mom did. Her husband was starting to get disturbed and Lenore was unhappy too. So she decided to force herself to improve. She made a rule that she could not go to Bible study if her house was not neat and clean by the time it was scheduled each week." Rosalie looked up from her food and smiled at me. "For some people that wouldn't be much of a consequence." She laughed. "But for Lenore Bible study class was important."

I nodded in agreement. "Yes," I said, "there needs to be a consequence that matters and a person needs to have a time goal like Lenore did."

"With that as her goal," Rosalie continued, "Lenore forced herself to learn how to keep the house nice. She discovered that the answer is to do regular, small amounts of cleaning each day.

"After twenty-six years of marriage, she still has the goal to straighten up before she starts the rest of the day." Rosalie sounded incredulous. "But," she added, "it takes her a half hour at most. Her three children help keep things nice around the house and are responsible for their own rooms.

"She uses the dinner meal as a focal point for the family for the day, giving everybody a job to do to prepare dinner. She said it's fun to work together as a family. That's why she includes everybody both for setting the table and cleaning up. Our family has had fun working together too," Rosalie added. "And I was glad to hear Lenore say it's become a heritage for them, something her family cherishes and the children will pass down to their families.

"She said Daniel, who's eleven, puts on the napkins and silverware. Darlene is a senior in high school. She puts on the plates and condiments. Michael puts on the drinks and coasters when he's home from college. Lenore puts the hot dishes on the counter and her husband, Jim, or someone else puts the food on the table with a serving spoon and trivet. Of course none of these jobs are hard but it's a big job for one person. Believe me, I know!"

Rosalie hurried on. "But Lenore said the point is not that she gets help. The point is it begins to focus the family as they stop other activities to help. She said everybody looks forward to getting together for the evening meal. Because of their meal chores, they are all there when the food is ready and can sit down right away to eat.

"To tell you the truth," Rosalie said to me, interrupting her own story, "I was amazed to see in action what we had been talking about. It had never occurred to me before we started these meetings to use housework for such a positive purpose."

I could tell that the visit had a significant impact on Rosalie. She continued telling me what Lenore had shared with her.

Clean-up

"Lenore explained that since there are only four of them at home now, they use a plan where everybody clears his own plate and silverware and whatever is on the table in front of him or her into the dishwasher. That way the table is cleared by the time everyone leaves the room. Of course, Lenore makes sure the dishwasher is empty before dinner. She usually finishes up the kitchen and starts the dishwasher but if she's tired, she asks somebody else to do it. She made it a point to say she's taught the children from the time they were three or four years old how to scrape plates, where to put them, how to carry dishes without spilling, and things like that.

"When they had two exchange students in the house, making six at the table, she used a different system where a team of two worked together to clean the table and kitchen. Sometimes it was boys' night, then girls' night, parents' night, or other combinations. If anyone was not going to be home for dinner on their night to clear, it was their responsibility to trade off with somebody else.

"The young ones learned from working with the older ones. Lenore said it made them feel grown up and included.

"She has a great incentive for them. They gather for dessert every night, even if it is just a cookie or piece of candy. It's become another family tradition. But they never have it until after the kitchen is cleaned up. The ones who aren't doing the kitchen use that in-between time to clean up their rooms."

Rosalie said she thought she had thrown Lenore a zinger when she asked her what she would do if a child just refused to cooperate, like stamping his or her foot and refusing to pick up toys, for instance. "As usual, Lenore didn't hesitate to answer," Rosalie said. "Lenore explained that everything has a consequence. Her kids have actually rebelled, and then Lenore gets a garbage bag and starts picking up toys. She tells them that if they don't take care of their toys by putting them away, she will give them to someone who will take care of them. She does a tricky thing, though. She starts with the broken stuff first to give the kids time to pick up the good toys before she gets to them. They can't get the toys out once they are in the bag. They are given away. Lenore said that's an absolute rule."

Rosalie seemed surprised at Lenore's commitment to following through on consequences. "Lenore has it right," I said. "Using swift, fair consequences consistently—and *consistently* is the key word—cuts down on a lot of struggle. Setting up a home that works well without a lot of hassle because children know where the boundaries are is a gift parents can give to their family."

Family Routines

When Rosalie asked about the kids cleaning their rooms, Lenore told her that the children's responsibilities grew as they grew. "At first, they would do a little while I worked in their rooms," Lenore said. "As they grew, they did more and I did less."

Rosalie went on, "Her husband used to do room inspections. Sometimes it even included the closets, but the kids would know that in advance. She said they do an overhaul of the closets twice a year, once before Christmas to make room for new things, and once at the beginning of the summer just because the children are home and have time to do it."

"I interrupted Lenore there," Rosalie said. "I couldn't believe she had such a head full of schedules that she was using every day. She surprised me with her response. She said they didn't really have schedules. They just have routines that make the family life flow without putting anybody under stress. They like to work together as a family, each doing his or her part.

"She said Darlene does all laundry for the whole family. She wanted a job to make some money. Lenore offered her several jobs, and she chose laundry. She is paid for doing the laundry. They change the sheets every two weeks and use one towel a week. Everybody has his own color with his name on it—like us." Rosalie smiled. "They have to hang up their towels after each use to make sure they dry in this Florida dampness.

"I couldn't believe that Lenore has never done laundry since she's been married. Her husband did it until Darlene took it over. When the children were too young to help, she had a woman clean every two weeks.

"They always try to have extra jobs around the house that enable the kids to earn money if they want to. She thought that this summer Jim would probably start training Daniel to do the lawn so he can earn money that way. It's great how they keep training and delegating themselves out of jobs," Rosalie said, laughing. "I guess it's good for them and good for the kids.

"By the way," Rosalie continued. "Darlene doesn't have to fold all that laundry. The family rotates that job. They have a stack of kind of long, colored blocks with each person's name on a block. When Darlene brings a load of clothes into the family room, she puts the block onto the top of the unfolded clothes pile in the laundry basket so that when the designated person comes into the family room, he or she sees the name and is reminded to fold the clothes. And there is a time limit too. If they don't get it done that day they have to fold two loads in a row.

"Lenore told me that one of her favorite stories is 'The Little Red Hen.' She said, 'You remember how the little red hen tried to get people to help her do all the things necessary to make bread but nobody would help her? She had to do all the work herself. When she finally baked a wonderful loaf of bread, everybody who had refused to work wanted a piece but she wouldn't give them any because they hadn't helped with the work. That's the approach we take,' she said. As a family, they share the work as well as the rewards of the work."

Rosalie paused in the story to collect her thoughts. She had learned a lot and it was hard to know what to tell next. A small run-down lobster boat, traps piled on its deck, chugged into port to a dock next to the restaurant dock. We watched it go by, leaving a whiff of fishy smells and whitish ripples in its wake. Then Rosalie continued.

Building a Way of Life

"I was getting a whole new view of how families work. This was not at all what I had expected. Where were the chore charts with mother working hard to check off things? Where was the scolding and punishment for not doing jobs? Where was the daily struggle to keep the house from getting out of control? All of that was strangely missing. I asked for more detail about how long all of this takes to get done each week, and Lenore said it doesn't take much time at all. Lenore thinks it's important for a child to have a little something to do each day like keep his or her room in order and helping at dinnertime.

"It has become their way of life. She said that over the years, she has taught one skill at a time, implemented it, and moved on to the next skill. She evaluates the children's skills from time to time and works on the ones that need improvement, like problems with hanging up towels or making the bed. It's obvious that she's teaching more than skills. She's teaching a way of life by just building a simple routine and following it.

"Lenore's children really don't have too many chores. For instance, her eleven year old just has to keep his room clean and help with setting and clearing the table at dinner every day. That's all for his daily chores. He does have a hampster he feeds several times a week but that is not a household chore. That was a choice he made for himself.

"He has three jobs a week. On Saturday he mops the tile floors in the entrance hall, the family room, and kitchen. After Darlene sweeps them, he just goes over them with a damp sponge mop. That takes about twenty minutes. If there is a soiled spot, he may have to take a little more time and work on that. He cleans the downstairs bathroom. That takes about ten minutes. And he takes the garbage to the curb twice a week. How long can that take? Five minutes?

"Darlene sweeps the tile and vacuums the rugs in the whole house on Saturday. She doesn't have to vacuum anybody's room if their floor is not clear. It takes her about forty-five minutes total to do a thorough job. Sometimes, if she is pressed for time, she can give it a quickie in about twenty minutes. She also does the upstairs bathroom.

"If they are going to be busy on Saturday, Lenore lets them do their jobs on Friday or Sunday.

"Lenore dusts the living areas when they need it during her half hour morning cleanup. Sometimes she does detail work, like shining bathroom fixtures and the kitchen sink or cleaning spots from heavily used areas, like the front doorjamb. That sounds pretty easy to me!"

As the sun began to lower over the bay, Rosalie looked at me with a puzzled expression. "I'm confused," she said. "I read somewhere that housework takes something like thirty-five hours a week, yet Lenore has a system that makes it seem like an easy job.

"I asked Lenore plainly about that. 'It seems like you're telling me that nobody works very hard around this house,' I said.

"Her answer was characteristically clear—and surprising. She said they don't work hard at all. Each of them does a little. The house never gets extremely messy. Because the children know they are part of the cleanup, they are more careful not to make messes that they or their siblings will have to clean up later.

"Even fixing dinner doesn't take her long, only about thirty minutes because she plans her menu every two weeks. She looks at her calendar to see what days are going to be busy and she fixes something easy on those days. In the morning, she looks to see what they're hav-

ing and puts something out to thaw. She plans only
one hard dish to fix per meal and has easy things to go
with it. She said if Jim is grilling outside, she may fix
french fries, which are time consuming. She wouldn't
go to all that trouble if she were making smothered
steak. In that case, she would put on baked potatoes
because they are easy. About once a week she fixes a
casserole early in the day so she doesn't have to do
much except heat it up with a few other easy things. It
all makes so much sense," Rosalie said. Then she
quoted Lenore. "The key to it all is to make it a point
to plan ahead."

I nodded in agreement, pleased with all Rosalie had
learned.

Rosalie pulled her thoughts back to our seaside loca-
tion and looked around, hoping the waitress was bringing our dessert.

"What she had to tell me next was probably the most
important thing of all. It was the backbone of her family plan," she said.

The waitress brought us the key lime pie we had
ordered. I was glad to see it was the authentic thing,
with regular crust, yellow filling, and egg white meringue.
Nothing compares with the creamy tart goodness of the
real thing, created by Conchs, the natives of the Florida
Keys.

The restaurant tables were now full of patrons waiting for the evening show—the sunset that was beginning to show signs of gathering its full color for display.
We ate quietly, savoring each rich bite. I didn't even think
about the calories. There are times just to savor the
moment, the scenery—and the key lime pie!

As Rosalie resumed telling me what Lenore had said,
I pressed my finger into a few last crust crumbs and
licked them unashamedly.

Family Bonding

"This wonderful thing happened as Lenore was raising her children," Rosalie said. "It turned out to be one of the most important things she did as a mother, and she sort of stumbled onto it. I'm sure it's the main reason they work so well together as a team. And it all started out because Lenore wanted to teach her children about the Bible.

"She knew that the best way to get children's interest was through play and acting out things, so she thought up all these games and crafts to get them interested in the Bible. For instance, they would bake bread together because the Bible talks a lot about bread. Jesus said, 'I am the bread of life' and 'A little leaven leavens the whole lump.' They would talk about what a certain passage means while they baked the bread. Sometimes they pulled a verse out of a box and talked about it, but usually they did something active.

"Here's another example. One night before dessert, they did a funny thing. She and her husband told the children that they were going to lead them in calisthenics. Jim started doing jumping jacks and Lenore started doing push-ups. Of course the children didn't know who to follow. They were illustrating the Bible verse, 'No man can serve two masters.' Isn't that clever? They taught them that you have to choose who you want to follow. You can't follow both at once.

"Another time they made pizza. Everybody chose different toppings and they used this to show how God has made everybody different with different tastes, abilities, and characteristics.

"They made puppets and put on skits. It sounds like their family has had a lot of fun. And the reason they started it was because they wanted the children to experience God in everyday life and to know how to talk about him. The activities had the unexpected effect of bonding the family very close together. It built a strong family. Lenore said it's easier to go through disagreements, hard times, and sorrows together because they have shared so much joy and fun together.

"Lenore believes that having the house organized allows them to build memories together. She said, 'As the adult woman leader of our family, I have more important contributions to make to our family than cleaning house. It is a waste of my time to focus on struggling with picking up what other people have dropped, battling back clutter made by uncooperative kids, fussing about messes, and doing work others can and should do. That's why we make it a team effort.' I love that philosophy!" Rosalie said.

"Lenore's daughter actually told her that when she has her own family and children, she wants to do the same things they did as a family. Lenore says she didn't do it for a heritage. She did it to teach them, but it turned into more than that.

"So," Rosalie said, smiling at me. "Thanks for sending me to Lenore's house. I learned that the most important thing is for the family to share in everything—the fun and the jobs that keep the house in order. They work as a team and obviously love it. But I'm sure it's Lenore's effort that has made it happen."

Rosalie and I sat listening to the steel drums and watching the setting sun begin to cast its red glow on the low clouds and reach up for the high ones. It was a lovely moment. In the background we heard the tune with the words about leaving a little girl in Kingston Town. I saw Rosalie's lips move and I thought I heard her say softly, "Help me, God."

I knew we would not meet again until after the summer was passed.

Yes, I thought, *please help her, God.*

ELEVEN

The Year in Review

If it's to be, it's up to me.

It had been just about a year since Rosalie and I had begun to meet together. We had not met over the summer and I suspected this would be the last time we would get together. Her "training" was just about over. We chose the Indian restaurant we had enjoyed before. It was quiet, and we had a certain privacy there. Besides, Rosalie was in the mood for spicy food. I had never seen her look so buoyant as she came through the door. She did not seem to have gained weight but her face looked more relaxed and fuller. She walked with a spring in her step and her eyes shone with enthusiasm. It was October. Summer had not yet loosened its hot hand on the days but the nights were getting cooler. We had the promise of better days to come.

"It's been a long time," I said. "It's good to see you! You certainly look chipper. Does that mean things are going well at your house?"

"Ah, that's a long story," she said. "Let's order and I will tell you about it."

We ordered the same things as before with Rosalie asking the waiter to make it a bit hotter than the "hot" category. Then she gave me the highlights of her past few months.

Working for a Dream

"We have made important strides this summer," she said. "But it wasn't easy. I'll spare you the usual family problems like Kerry breaking his finger at summer camp or the awful dog we babysat for friends on vacation. Never again! We went on vacation and had summer fun. But that's not what I really want to get to!

"Here's what has happened with the house. I kept setting systems in place for organizing. I made changes a little at a time and checked to make sure they were going well before I added anything else. We read the family reminders at the table pretty regularly. That's a really good idea, you know! Of course, we posted the motto and made sure everyone could pronounce it and remembered it meant 'Seek to excel.'

"One of the things I kept uppermost in my mind was to keep telling the kids and Ben how great things were going to be when we got things working automatically. I wanted to keep the vision before them because I remember you saying that people will work for a dream but not to solve problems. I made sure they knew I was aware of all of the good changes each of them was making. And I made sure I talked to them individually.

"I started keeping a notebook about our conversations and special things I could do for them to let them know they were important members of the family in every way, not just for work. Interacting with my kids in this way has made me more sensitive to them as individuals.

"I went to a concert with Becky and her friends. I was surprised they even wanted me to go. It was not my cup of tea but I learned a lot about Becky and her friends and I think they all appreciated my interest. Maybe it was because I paid for treats after the concert!" she said, laughing a little.

"I went fishing with Bill and Kerry. You know what? They become different people when they fish—so much more mature when they are in charge, the experts. We got stuck in mud on the way back and that was a hilarious adventure.

"Jo turned five in August and we—but you don't want to know the details of how I am really trying to bond more with my kids. I can see that what you said is true. Family bonding really is the glue that holds this whole organizing thing together."

Rosalie was leaning forward. Her hands and face were animated as she poured out the story of how her management ideas had changed her life. Then she continued.

"I bought a book on family crafts and games you suggested and we have started doing fun activities together. You know, I wouldn't have had the time or energy for that kind of thing before we had this teamwork approach to the house. Sometimes these activities match the lessons they are learning at church and sometimes they are just things I think they need to think about. Sometimes they go along with the holidays. We made a cake together for the Fourth of July and decorated it like a flag. We talked about the meaning of the colors and why we have the number of stars and stripes we do. We had a good time doing it.

"Wearing our family T-shirts and displaying our motto has helped too.

"Sometimes we slipped back. We had our rocky places. Billy decided he wasn't going to bathe or wash clothes anymore at all. Ben had to handle that little problem. And that was good because he is working to have a more meaningful relationship with the kids too. I used that as an opportunity to reevaluate whether I need to work on my managerial skills.

"Beth decided her room was her own, and I should have no say in how she keeps it, so we had to negotiate a satisfactory approach that we could both live with. She is getting older and will soon be making all of her decisions about how she wants to live. I guess we have to make adjustments as the children mature and take on more responsibilities for their own lives. I think we are closer as a result of this 'course correction' we had to make.

"I taught the three older kids to wash their own clothes, and I put a hamper in each of their rooms. One day Kerry decided bleach would be a good idea and now he has speckled jeans. That was the same week he cut a chunk out of his hair. That boy is getting way too old for that!"

On and on she went, telling the new ideas she had implemented. She told how she handled challenges and celebrated victories. I smiled as I dipped the flat roti bread into yogurt and onion relish.

"I think I already know the answer, but how is Rosalie doing?" I asked when she came to a stop.

A Changed Life

"The Rosalie you see before you is a different Rosalie from the one you met about this time last year. I'm not saying I have arrived. I see so much more to be done, but now I know how to do it.

"Of all the things we discussed, I think that when I finally caught a vision of what a real family could and should be, my life was changed. Once I knew where we were going as a family and why, there was no going back! I think it was the trip to Lenore's house that did the trick. I had one of those aha! moments. I realized for the first time what family teamwork really means, that family life could be really fun! It was a real revelation."

I saw that Rosalie wasn't talking so much to me as to herself, cherishing the miracles, the revelations, the experiences of the heart and mind that she had discovered over the past year. Her mothering spirit had been unleashed and was soaring beyond her original idea of having a neater house and more cooperative family. She had discovered truths she never dreamed existed. She knew there was wealth within her waiting to be discovered, ideas and imaginations that would flow from her into her family for generations to come. She felt the presence of God in it all.

She spoke of how life runs on rules, joyful rules, about details of how many towels to use, who sets the table and when, how we clear the table, and where we put the dishes. These were not restrictions. They were details that moved the family from mere existence to quality life together—the life of excellence they were seeking together.

She recounted how she had been required to transform herself from a "can-do" kind of a gal, who tackled a job when she saw it, into a long-range planner, who lives proactively with a dream in mind. Before, she had procrastinated and then rushed ahead with frenzied work. Now, she had learned to be a more consistent manager. She had learned to live mindfully in the moment, to notice details of how the house looked and how each person was doing with his or her chores and in life in general. Rosalie compared herself to a caterpillar turning into a butterfly and said that although sometimes it was taxing to fly so far and wide, she wouldn't become an earthbound caterpillar again for anything.

A True Manager

It was her view that the whole thing has to do with really caring about the right things. Then everything else falls into place. Supervising her team members in keeping the systems she had set up was an expression of her caring. As long as the system was in place, the family was free to be the family, not just a network of individuals, bumping into each other as they lived their lives in the same house. She said that she had to make sure she kept her heart open to caring and not withdraw back into just wanting the house to be in order.

Rosalie told me something she had never shared before. She and Ben had begun sitting down together every two or three months and discussing their relationship, the children, and the house. They kept a journal, or minutes if you will, of how the family was doing. They recorded the strengths of each child they needed to compliment and the weaknesses they needed to work on. Together they devised plans to tackle the problems. They discussed their marriage and changes they could make to improve it. They evaluated the needs of the house, things that could be improved and when and how they would make the improvements. I could see that Rosalie had moved beyond our discussions. She was truly the manager now and had begun her own innovations and systems.

Another of the innovations she had begun was a systems folder that described how the house was run. There were pages for the finances, which told how much money they had and where it was kept, and pages with information on monthly bills and their budget. These pages told where the receipts were to be kept and how the credit card reports were to be gone over and when.

The systems folder explained the dinner routine. It included the "In this family, we . . ." list that she read from nightly. It contained the plans she had made for laundry and cleaning. It had pictures and written descriptions of what each room should look like. It had instructions on exactly how to do jobs like mopping the kitchen floor and cleaning the bathroom.

Rosalie said she could remember many of these things but when they were written into a systems folder, they became more real, more important. They seemed to mean more to the family than if they existed only in her mind. If they were written, they were more official.

She wondered if the main strength of the systems folder might be that it forced her to think out exactly what she wanted to do and how she wanted it done. As time went by, systems became interwoven with everyday life and became the background on which the family painted their daily-living pictures. The systems folder took its place in family lore, family culture. They now worked to meet the expectations written there. Organized living became easier because it became automatic.

Rosalie said it was easier to coast through life as she had been doing earlier but, oh the joy of being on an upward path to an important place! She had caught the significance of her place in the world. God had given her a mission, and she was delighted to have been entrusted with it. She wanted the family to live up to its full potential. Then all of the members would have a chance to reach their own reason for being in the world. She is leaving a heritage.

Achieving the Dream

Then, as Rosalie talked, she turned her attention beyond her own walls. She mused that if everybody who was living in the shadows as she had been were suddenly enlightened, they would follow the same core principles of clarity, consistency, and bonding. But they would apply them in so many different ways. She reflected that her house was not the same as Lenore's or mine, but we are all on the same track of using systems that work for us to move us and our families forward. Each family is unique and special in its own way. Yet each of us is striving to reach its fullest potential.

"It's up to the Manager to achieve the dream of the Visionary," she said with conviction.

Rosalie stopped to drink her hot chai before she continued. "Our house is changing as we change. We are a different family from the one we were a year ago. I'm a family developer, a child mentor. I finally woke up to my place in this whole picture—what the title Mom really means when it comes to managing a home. It definitely doesn't mean a full-time, hardworking, grumbling, tired maid, like I thought before. About time I figured that out, I'd say! We just had our twentieth wedding anniversary. Beth is almost eighteen!" She looked pensively away through the window to the passing traffic and sighed.

I waited a moment to honor her reverie. "You woke up earlier than I did," I said. "You are experiencing the regrets many of us do when we realize what we should have been doing all along. Don't worry about catching up. Just keep going from where you are now.

"Don't sell yourself short either. Beth has learned a valuable lesson you may have not been able to teach any other way. She has seen how a person can catch a vision, design a way to make that dream come true, and follow through with those plans. Maybe that is the most valuable lesson of all."

TWELVE

A Letter to Rosalie

Do not keep anything in your home that you do not know to be useful or believe to be beautiful.

William Morris

Dear Rosalie,

Time passes faster than we realize. For a whole year we have met together! You learned a lot and so did I. Our meetings forced me to organize the ideas we discussed in a way I never would have otherwise.

It is important that you integrate what we learned into a whole, well-rounded picture. From our last conversation, it looks like you are well on the way to doing that. To test where you are in your journey, pretend a visitor comes to your door. This is an unusual visitor, because from her head are two antennae. As she enters, her antennae angle and turn in order to take in every aspect of your home. She notices the decor—colors, textures, style of furniture, how it all works together on a visual level. She evaluates the cleanliness and orderliness of the house. She senses an atmosphere of beauty and serenity.

Furthermore, she senses the smells of the house. Fresh or floral-scented, bleach or pine cleanser. Her antennae pick up the voices of children, music playing, and television wafting from various family rooms.

Finally, she focuses on the people in the home. She notices the look on your face, the tone of your voice. She perceives the silent interplay between members of the family, not only with each other but with the way things are run in the house. Nothing escapes her attention. Her active antennae make it impossible for her to ignore any part of your home.

These are the perceptions of the visitor's conscious mind. They take place without her even realizing it because her sensory intake is so automatic and habitual. The perceptions are transferred to her inner core through the antennae where they are processed without her brain's reflecting on them. She is not even aware of the process.

But the real action is in the visitor's unconscious mind. There reside your visitor's personality, needs, expectations, beliefs, past experiences, and attitudes. The information sent to it from the conscious mind is processed to answer one question: Does this house and family meet my need? If the answer is yes, you receive the designation of home from that visitor. If the answer is no, your visitor is uncomfortable and wants to leave.

That visitor is you, Rosalie, and each member of your family, as you enter the house. Each minute you spend in the house, you are processing in a hundred different ways how the home you have created meets your needs. Your family members are doing the same. All of the details, rules, systems, and the like create the atmosphere you want your family to experience.

You have some leeway because your family is bound together by shared history, habit, and love. They have forgiven you many errors and will forgive many in the future, just as you have forgiven them. But at this point in history with stresses pulling you and your family apart, you need to create a home that, in a thousand unconsciously perceived ways, loudly says home to them.

When I saw you walk away from our last visit, I thought I knew where you would be going. But as I reflected on it, I realized I didn't know anything of the sort. You have a thousand decisions ahead of you. How could I begin to guess exactly how you will proceed? You have already surprised me with your own innovations. But I think I do know one thing. You will go with a different attitude from the one you had when you came to me. Somehow over this year you have found your spirit.

The curtain of your understanding has lifted and you see yourself as a part of God's big and wonderful plan for your life and the life of your family. The curtain of your heart has lifted, and you are willing to open yourself to caring and love in a specific way you did not before. The curtain of your mind has lifted and you see routines, rules, and systems not as a nuisance to be endured but a path to harmony and dignity.

Organizing your home has caused you to test all of the assumptions you had about yourself, your family, and your life. Fuzzy generalizations have given way to clear practicalities. Your "work harder and hope for the best approach" that didn't work has been traded in for specific plans that do. You have found out who you and your family really are. On that information you have created an important world of your own, one that bridges the gap from the earthly to the eternal.

My final word may seem a strange one. It is this: Remember your systems. Never again slip into casual mindlessness. Decide where you want to go with your family and mindfully develop specific ways to get there. Hoping, however sincere, won't do it. Apply your systems intelligently, prayerfully, reasonably, intentionally, and compassionately.

I am reluctant to let you go. Our relationship has been very meaningful to me. My heart goes with you as you follow your spirit down the path before you. Let me know how you are doing and where your spirit leads.

Warmly,

Sandra Felton

Helpful Letters from Moms in the Trenches

These letters are not from experts, just from moms who are expressing their problems and reaching out to help each other on groups linked from the www.messies.com web site. They are not in any special order. Each has been chosen because it expresses the topic well, whether describing difficulties or sharing things they have found that work.

Abbreviations are very much part of the e-mail culture. Dh is "dear husband" (I suspect sometimes it is "darn husband"), dd4 is "four-year-old dear daughter." BTW is "by the way" and LOL means "laughing out loud." MV stands for Mount Vernon, which is a decluttering method used by Messies Anonymous. I tell about this in *The New Messies Manual* and on my web site.

No attempt has been made to clean up the writing. E-mail often is very casual and does not follow standard English-teacher grammar rules. In these postings, you are peeking into the windows of the women's lives. Use what you like.

She's Given Up

I truly am not a messy person at heart . . . but I've given up on many things when I had kids. Having a clean house is one. With the two little ones I have now, the constant fighting and destruction they cause is beyond me. I'm trying different tactics to reach them, and get them to at least pick up after themselves. And to respect property and other people . . . we are making slow, but steady progress.

It seems that no matter what, I am solely responsible for everything, and there are no excuses. It doesn't matter whether I'm sick, depressed, worked 20 hours straight, and have another 4 appointments to run, or if the kids just dumped a box of cereal on the floor and the box of toys, I'm still responsible.

My time at home is very limited; when I work, I have about 3 to 5 hours a day with my kids and most of that, I must spend cleaning up after them, running errands, and maintain my sanity.

Her Mom Made It Look Easy

My mom, though strict in other areas, was kind of easy on my brother and me when it came to doing housework (though we were expected to do more than I expect of my boys). We had to keep our own rooms picked up and clean them every Saturday (as does my oldest—we MV'd his room in the spring, but 10 yr. old's is still a disaster zone, and there are no flat surfaces visible to clean!) As we got older, my brother mowed the lawn (as does my 14 yr. old), and I helped with dusting, sweeping, dishes, etc. (my 10 yr. old does like to sweep when we can get to the floor! LOL). My mom was a cleanie and made it look so easy, I never realized how much there was to do. When I got married at age 20, what a rude awakening! I had never realized how much work it was to keep house because she had made it look so effortless (still does). She also didn't like people in "her" kitchen, so my cooking skills were very limited (poor hubby was my guinea pig!).

Anyway, I want my boys to have the basic life skills, so I have my work cut out for me, as oldest is only four years away from college now! I have to say, they are both very good boys, and basically don't help much because I haven't trained them to do so. Thanks again for your advice.

Making Plans Ahead

Since my son is still young I do not currently have him helping me do much but I plan to when he is older and that is part of why I want to get myself organized now. I think it is very important that kids be taught how to do all the housework so they know how to when they have their own house and also to help out with daily chores. They make plenty of extra work for us so it is only right for them to help out with as much as they can. When I was a kid I really resented doing any housework I had to do so I think it will be tricky starting out with them but soon they will be able to see how easy it is and how capable they are. I can think of lots of questions to ask you and ideas on how to get started teaching your boys but I do not want to sound preachy since I have no actual experience.

So here are just a couple to get started and then if you want more you can ask me for more. Your ten year old may be young enough to still use a chart for chores and get a reward at the end of the week and you can also tie privileges to chores for your 14 year old. They can be made to at least do self-care for their own items such as school books, sports equipment, toys, etc. Then they can have privileges removed or given as reward if they accomplish this. Then as they do those regularly they can also do household chores—laundry, vacuuming, dishes—whatever. Especially say Saturday morning before they are allowed to go anywhere for the day they should do their work first.

Okay—that is enough and I am rambling. Hope this has been a little bit helpful. This all sounds great till my own kids are that age. I hope that I can get them trained to help out as much as I currently dream about!

About Cooking

To my beloved Cooking Buddies: I actually went grocery shopping yesterday, bought some good hamburger on sale, and not only made myself grilled burgers for dinner, but made a meatloaf with the rest of the ground beef, bread that wasn't quite sandwich-quality anymore, the rest of the open jar of salsa, and one egg. I'm having some of it for lunch, so it's even edible!! I am still pinching myself to see if I am dreaming. I have only been to McDonald's once this week, and my son hasn't been at all. He hasn't complained—he just likes to go play in the McDonaldland Playplace anyway, so we will do that after lunch tomorrow (eating at home). We'll just buy a soda each, and he will go play with the other kids in the Playplace for half an hour while I sit and watch him. $2.00 is much more doable than the $8.00 we were spending two or three times a week!

Needs Cleaning Advice

I know the reason I am messy is mostly due to motivational, emotional, disorganizational reasons, however one thing that I realized and that I am kind of embarrassed to admit because it seems like it should be a "no brainer" and something every woman should know, but . . . ok . . . My Mom never TAUGHT me the right way to clean! I guess my way through the products/process of everything from toilets, appliances, whatever! Recently you all came to my rescue on how to clean my drip pans and that is what I am getting at. Now I am obsessed with my walls and baseboards. Is there any source out there that tells the proper and most effective way to clean every nook/cranny/object! Some of the things I attempt may be interpreted as being "half done/quick job/not thorough" but it is not that I am trying to be that way, I just don't know the best way to do it. Cleaning was always more of a discipline issue when I was growing up. If it wasn't done "right" it had to be redone along with a lot of angry hassle, threats, heartache, but I don't remember ever actually being taught the "right" way (unless I was being scolded or belittled in the process and tuned it out). My girls are 3 and 14 months.

I want to teach them the art of keeping a nice home from the start according to their age/abilities and something that we just do and then get on with the rest of our day. I want to teach them the right way and make it as "pleasant" an experience as chores can be and then the satisfaction of accomplishing those things. I don't want them to go through what I seem to struggle with every day of my life. Maybe if I teach them, I can learn with them and we can all benefit! Anyone know any house-cleaning 101 sources that touch on the actual process, not just getting yourself to do it? Your help would be GREATLY appreciated!!! Thanks!

Note: When moms are under stress, it is hard to see possibilities.

Toys Rule Her Life

Now for my problem: TOYS . . . I am afraid to say the word. Toys rule my life. I trip on them, I fall over them, they are coming out from under every piece of furni-ture. It is a horror story, I tell you. Our home is rather small and the kids' rooms are the smallest of all. We have no porch and although we have a huge backyard, I hate to leave anything out there for fear of sun, rain and wid-ows (black, esp.). Why do I not get rid of some and resell others at consignment??? I DO. But to be honest, most of this stuff is in PERFECT condition and I can not see the value in just getting rid of it all. I am not guilty of buy-ing all of it. Most of it comes from family, friends, etc. I try to have the kids help me decide what we no longer need, but even they have a hard time deciding. My 3 year old son will say "I need it all, mamma." My 7 year old daughter will say "I am just not sure what to save and what to get rid of, it's all so nice . . ."

Handling Toys

Well, I have 3 kids and this is what I do. I got rid of everything that you just look at and drop (like figures, toys that have a million parts, etc.). My 4 year old isn't into hero figures, doesn't watch TV or movies really so he's never had one of those super heroes. But anything they are too old for goes out immediately. We have such a small house and tons of stuff comes in from relatives, etc. and I only keep the best items. This past Christmas we got a lot of junky plastic toys from relatives and I just returned them at Walmart, etc. My kids don't know about it because I don't feel like they can be saddled down with making those kinds of decisions. I hate plastic junky toys and it's my job to keep the house semi neat and in order so we can have a smooth running family and homeschool at the same time (even so, it's a real struggle 100% of the time). It's still amazing how much stuff comes into the house like Sunday school stuff and daily drawings, etc. I don't ask them if they want to keep whatever, I just either throw it out or save it and if they don't mention it in a few days then I toss it. I also get rid of tons at Salvation Army. I know it sounds mean and really tough, but we have such a small house and books are taking over. My 10 year old is a big reader and my 8 year old is big on art so we have tons of books and art supplies.

We also have a rule about one thing out at a time, like one major toy or one craft item or game. I wouldn't allow LEGOs, Lincoln logs and a game all out at the same time. For one thing our house is way too small for that and we need walking space, and that teaches them to pick up after themselves. For the first several months you have to keep after them about it. I also make allowances like if one child wants to play with tinker toys and the other wants to do an art project, then that's OK as long as they pick up after themselves. So all this works for us anyway. Good luck!

Yelling (Not) at Kids

Yelling at our kids. Who hasn't done it?? It was starting to become a BIG problem for me. I hated it but somehow couldn't stop doing it (maybe it's that Italian blood?). My husband would mention how much I yelled at our daughter and tell me that she is only 4 and I shouldn't be so hard on her. I prayed every day to stop but it continued. (You're probably thinking at this point that this is off topic—but wait!!)

Once I stopped to think about when most of the yelling happened I started to see a pattern. I yelled when we were late (again) going somewhere. I yelled when my daughter made a big mess (again). I even yelled when she accidentally spilled something! She always complained about being tooooo tired to do the things that I asked of her.

Last night I realized that I haven't yelled at her all week! I know that it has been at least that long maybe a little longer. What has changed? Several things have.

First of all, I have been getting the clutter under control so the messes are less and I am less stressed all the time. Secondly, I started teaching my daughter routines. Before she goes to bed we clean up her room. (Yes, I stopped being a martyr and started helping out.) Everything is where it should be when she goes to bed. She wakes up in the morning and we make her bed immediately. She picks up her toys before she moves on to other things. She will ask me "Can I watch a video now?" and I will respond "Well, let's pick up these things first" and she will gladly do it. She used to whine and complain about this!

Thirdly, I started planning an extra 5–10 minutes for cleanup and straightening before we had to go anywhere. We started practicing on noncommittal events like going to the grocery store (no appointment time there!). I would set the timer and tell her that when it went off that we would have to go. The timer goes off and she's not quite ready, but we do have an extra 10 minutes to finish and straighten up!

The combination of all of these things has helped tremendously. When she has an accidental spill then I have found myself shrugging it off and sometimes even laughing. What a change! (I have bought her a hand-held vacuum cleaner so she can help with her messes.)

This has been such a blessing in our home. I don't think that she has realized it yet. I never realized how much clutter had ruled my life.

Living Room Cleanup

I thought I was the only one with a problem when it came to kids and their backpacks and other stuff in the living room. I think I have a secret fear of becoming the cleanie my mother was (a perfect 10). After getting the living room decent while the kids are in school, I feel great. By bedtime it looks like disaster again. I have occasionally filled up a laundry basket with stuff I have gathered from the living room and told them to sort it out when they got home. Sometimes this works. Now this is the weekend, I am going to ask them today to put their backpacks in their rooms. I'm not sure if it will work or not. I know when I was a student a few months ago, I left my backpack and books laying around so that I would know where they were. I think I just did not want to put forth the effort to walk to my room when I had to do my homework. At my house, the kids all sit around the living room to do their homework and this results in papers everywhere. Perhaps I need to put some kind of boundary on what I will accept in the living room. Kinda tough to do when I was guilty of doing the same thing not too long ago. Any suggestions?

Delegation

One of my biggest problems is delegation. I have two teenage girls. One is really messy and the other is semi. I think I just have too much to do. I do have time but I get tired cleaning up after everyone. There isn't any order and I feel like I'm drifting away. And I can't find the paddle.

Good Advice

I'm a mom of four, so I've been through this. You have my sympathy. Toddlers learn by dumping, exploring, and making messes. Be glad you have a smart and healthy baby. Don't drive yourself nuts chasing after her picking up. Don't have too many things where she can get at them; limit the amount she can get out to what you can put away in 5 minutes. (With my fourth child, I was so desperate I put locks on the toy cupboards, which sounds cruel. However, it not only helped me be a kinder and more patient mother and gave my family a pleasant house to live in, it also protected my baby from the older kids' Legos, etc. that she might choke on.) At this age, it may make sense to just have a pretty basket or container you can dump all the toys in quickly when it's clean-up time, but pretty soon (say, by 24 months), it makes sense to have shelves, with containers for multi-piece toys (preferably containers that your daughter chooses or decorates herself), because with all the toys just dumped together, she won't be able to find what she wants and she'll just have to make a mess to find things. (You want her to learn how pleasant it is to have order, because when you have order you can find what you want.)

Keep on top of your other housework as much as you can while still taking good care of her and yourself, and realize that you don't really have a messy house. You have a neat and clean house with a toddler playing in it! Then, maybe about three times a day, at a set time that your baby can learn to predict, and preferably before an activity that she likes, do a 5-minute cleanup. ("Now, we're going to put all the toys away so we can go to the park to ride the swings!" or "The toys need to go in their home so we can eat our lunch" or "Let's make the house pretty for Daddy.") Give her a warning about 5 minutes before it's going to begin, so it won't come as a terrible shock to her while she's in the middle of something. Try to make a game of it. It'll get easier as she gets older; at first, it'll just be you demonstrating how you put toys away, while she puts three things away and dumps out two. (You may even need to gently take her hand and physically teach her how to put something in the container.) Try to show by your attitude that cleanup is fun; don't get all tired and resentful about it, because then she'll learn cleanup is to be avoided if at all possible. Also, and this is hard to explain, don't expect her to make a sudden change; get into her rhythm and start where she is and move her to where you want her to be. In other words, if she is playing with animals, don't just swoop in and make her start cleaning up; begin by playing her game with her for a little bit, and then say something like, "Oh, Cow's hungry, she wants to go in her barn and have her dinner" and walk the cow over to where she belongs, and have her start munching and saying "Oh, thank you for bringing me to eat my yummy dinner." Then ask your little one, "Who else needs dinner?" (and hope she'll walk Pig over to where he belongs instead of saying "No! Wanna play!") Give your baby choices, when you can, such as which toys to put away first, and in what way. Let her feel in charge of her own cleanup, and she'll begin, very gradually, to take responsibility for it.

Be sure the toys get cleaned up at bedtime, because you don't want to wake up to a messy, discouraging house, and you don't want your husband to break his neck if he gets up to use the bathroom in the middle of the night.

Seventeen months is not too early for you to begin trying to teach her to clean up, but remember, it is a long slow process. Be patient. The sooner and more lovingly you can begin it, the sooner you'll actually have a little helper rather than a little mess maker. Don't get mad if she can't do it yet, and try to make it a delight for her. (Easier said than done sometimes, I know.) Every kid is different, and some are tidier by nature or more physically co-ordinated or intellectually advanced, so accept her just as she is, because she's doing the best she can, just like you are. However, at her age, she can probably be exposed to the idea of putting things away, she can "dust" (sort of) (my kids loved a dustcloth puppet that I made for them), she can use a whisk broom or sponge if you don't expect results, she can help sort laundry (this is even good for her intellectual development), and carry things around for you and feel like a big girl. She probably loves to play in water, so you can get her to wash things (which you will need to finish up afterwards if they really need to be clean). She will probably enjoy putting things in the hamper, but they may not all be dirty clothes! ("Oh, here's where Mama's glasses went!") Give her cleaning tools that are comfortable and safe for her to use, and give her lots of praise and encouragement, even if she isn't much help yet. Try to communicate clearly what you want from her, because the goals that are so obvious to you don't make any sense to her. Remember that at this age, babies love to "be like Mama," and they learn so much by imitation. (And they imitate not only your actions, but your spirit, so watch out!) Catch her now, while she still thinks it's fun to do what Mama does; it's a lot easier to keep her cleaning up than to try to start later when the imitating phase is past.

Set a good example by staying on top of your own jobs if you can, but remember nothing is more important than giving her what she needs at this age, so you might want to temporarily lower your standards, but don't lower them to a level that is going to make you or your husband unhappy, or that will allow the house to start a downward spiral. If there's any way to afford it, get household help. (I could only afford it one time in my life, but that $25 made such a difference to my attitude that it was worth it. I wish I could have done it more.) If there's any way your husband could give you more help, ask him; it's a way he can make a real contribution to the well-being of his little daughter.

It's normal for 17-month-olds not to have much attention span, and to take out lots of toys, but if she is always taking out another toy, it may be that the toys she has have become boring to her. Since babies crave learning more than almost anything else except love, she has the sense to keep looking when her toys don't give her what she needs. You could teach her a new way to play with the toys she has, get out some toys she hasn't seen for awhile, or get her new toys at a higher developmental level. Another thing I have noticed is that if there are too many toys available, or a chaotic environment with no spot of beauty, or a lot of conflict between the parents, or a TV going constantly, or if babies are physically unwell, sometimes babies have a hard time focusing on any one toy. I also found that when I paid more attention to my kids and made sure life was giving them enough interesting mental challenges, they had less need to make messes and less time to make them. So, instead of leaving my kids to play while I did the laundry, we did laundry together while I told them stories. Instead of leaving them to play while I vacuumed, they would use the dustbuster or ride on the vacuum cleaner. Instead of leaving them to play while I did mending, we did a craft project together (and I did the mending later, or did it while they were sewing with big plastic needles in Styrofoam meat trays, or sometimes I just said "Forget about the mending; THIS is what I'm home for!") I found that if you play their little games with them, often they can stick with the same toy for much longer than if they were playing alone, and you end up with less mess to clean up. My babies also "helped" me cook. As early as possible, I tried to get them in the habit of "First we all work together, and then we'll have time to play together." (Of course, a baby of 17 months doesn't have the mental or emotional ability to really defer gratification and wait; she wants what she wants right now, so you need to make the process of cleaning up work for her, too. It's not really going to motivate her that she can go to the zoo in an hour if she cleans up! It needs to be fun right NOW, or she won't want to do it.)

Another thing that helps is to spend as much time as you can manage comfortably in the "great outdoors." If you're not in the house, she can't be messing it up. (It's also true that then you can't be cleaning, but at this age they can mess up faster than we can clean up, so it's a net gain.) Also, being outdoors seems to make many babies more contented and helps them sleep longer, both of which are a big help to Moms who want nice homes. Being outdoors has also been known to improve a mom's own mood, and make her feel more able to cope with the stresses of raising a child this age.

Never turn cleanup into a contest of wills. She's just coming up on the age where she is beginning to learn "I am a separate person from Mama, and I can make choices and say 'NO!'" You'll be sorry if you let cleanup be the issue she chooses to assert her independence with, and it could make her grow up with the same Messie tendencies you and I struggle with.

At your library (or bookstore, but it may be out of print), look for the toddler picture book "Messy Baby" by Jan Ormondroyd. It will give you a chuckle. In it, you see the dad going around the house tidying and the baby follows along behind messing things up.

Give yourself a big pat on the back. You are doing the hardest, most important work in the world. Enjoy your baby, and remember that "this too shall pass."

(Sorry this has been so long.)

Home

Anne, the KEY to training your kids is consistency! Your kids are at the perfect age to train, because they LOVE to "help." It makes them feel "BIG." My two year old is much better about picking up after himself than his big brother and sister (who WERE trained when they were young, but got out of their previous good habits when my dh and I reconciled after a 3 year separation. He didn't like to see them doing chores and wouldn't let me punish them if they didn't do what they were supposed to do).

If you want to train your children to good habits, you really have to be close enough at hand and keep an eye out on what they are doing during playtime until they are in the habit. Fortunately, at that age, it really doesn't take them long to catch on.

Are you/they on any type of schedule or routine?? If so you can just have them clean up when they are done with their playtime. I get down on the floor with my son and sing the "clean up song" from Barney and start putting things back in his toy box. I will tell him, pick up your truck and put it in the bucket, pick up your hammer, your bunny, etc. and get specific, until every item is in the bucket. Put up your books on the shelf, etc. Then I praise him lavishly. After bath time, I tell my son to put up his toys in the basket (I have one of those 3 tier veggie baskets hanging from the shower head to store his toys in). He can reach the bottom two baskets, but he hands me the ones that won't fit in the lower ones and I put them in the basket for him.

It helps a great deal if you don't have an overwhelming number of toys at one time available to them to drag out. If that is the case, I would sort out the toys into 2 or 3 storage boxes and only keep one out for a week or so, then put it up and get down the others. That way they will get more use out of the toys because by rotating them around they are like "new" toys again and they aren't bored with them. Toys with lots of little pieces like puzzles, Legos, Duplos, Tinkertoys, Mr. Potato Head, etc, I keep them in separate containers and store them where they do not have free access to them. I will get them down for play when I can kinda be on hand and make sure that they are picked up when they want to go onto something else. We home school the older 2, so I will let my 2 year old play with these while we work in the other part of the room. When he gets tired of playing with them, I will have him put them all back into the container where they go before I allow him to play with anything else.

When my kids spill something, I give them a rag and tell them to wipe it up. Even my 2 year old knows now without being told and will go and get a rag himself. Of course he doesn't do a thorough job, but he is getting trained in the idea that he is responsible for cleaning up his mess. When he finishes a snack or meal, or a drink, I tell him to put the dishes in the sink. When he has some trash, I tell him to go put it in the garbage. When I change his clothes or undress him for the tub, I hand him his clothes and tell him to put them in the hamper. When I change his diaper, I let him dispose of it (not the #2 diapers, though!). And so on. Just do it as you go, consistently and they will catch on quickly with just a little effort on your part. My two year old is constantly scolding his big brother and sister when they leave their clothes on the floor and don't pick up their mess!

As for other cleaning—the BEST thing you can do at this stage of your life is to simplify, simplify, simplify!! Cut down on dustbuster knick knacks, put throws over your upholstered furniture, get rid of that kitchen counter clutter, store as few things on any horizontal surface in your home as you possibly can. Remove anything that is high-maintenance if you can. Sit down and figure out exactly WHAT is the bare minimum that you can do each day to maintain. Keep the list down to about 10 items. Then figure out what you need to do each week and distribute them throughout each day of the week OR if you can, set aside one day a week to attend these chores when you can have a baby-sitter or someone else watch your kids. (Mother's day out programs were a lifesaver to me when my older two kids were that age!)

Another thing I do is to separate chores I can do when the kids are awake and things that I can do when they are not around. Things like washing dishes, cooking and surface cleaning in the kitchen I can do with my son right there. He might be using canned goods as building blocks, banging the pots and pans or playing with the Tupperware, but that is easily put back and keeps him occupied. What I did with my kids was to sacrifice a bottom cupboard in the kitchen and put a little bit of stuff in there like an old percolator, and kitchen odds and ends and toys. That was "his" cabinet. If you are dusting, put an old white sock on their hands and let them "help." Give them a small hand broom and dustpan and let them sweep under the table while you do something else close by. When you are bathing the kids, let them play a bit in the tub while you surface clean and disinfect the fixtures. We have one of those upright vacuums with the built in hose and my son LOVES to "vacuum" with the hose while I am pushing around the upright.

For things that you cannot do with them awake and afoot—mopping is on that list—either wake up early and do them before they get up in the AM or after they go to bed at night. I would discourage you from doing them while they are napping—use that time to rest yourself or relax with a project you enjoy or talk on the phone, read, etc. I also try to do certain tasks when their favorite TV program is on or pop in a video and they are distracted without making a mess.

But remember the key here is CONSISTENCY when training. You have to make sure they do it EVERY time—even if you have to discipline them. But if you make it fun and like a game—oh I bet I can beat you picking up the blocks—you won't have to. Also a routine of some sort will help immensely, too. Believe me, it WILL get easier; you will get to put the knobs back on your stove one day, just hang in there and TRAIN now!!

I hope this helps!!

Doing the Daily Chores

I am a SAHM of 2 girls ages 4 and 1/2 and 13 months. The older one knows the rule "You can only have one toy/book out at a time. When you want to play with something else then you have to put the last item away ... If you're not playing with it, then put it away." I get her to repeat it often. I use nap times, snack times, lunch time, dinnertime, and bedtime as benchmarks for cleaning up stuff. i.e.—they don't get to eat their lunch until things are picked up. You may have to help a lot in the beginning but they will start to get the hang of it as long as you're consistent. DD4 has now started to ask me if she can play with a certain toy before she goes and gets it out. This has been a great transformation in our house. This has been done with about 6 weeks of consistent reminders. As I have been more aware of the stuff, it has made it easier to see it all (as it happens).

I have one major cleaning day a week (Monday). DD4 knows that Monday is cleaning day. Mom is not available to entertain!! She actually likes helping me clean. I have sometimes had to be creative with the chores but she loves to help. The other days of the week I have strict daily chores which don't take any longer than 45 minutes in the morning and 45 minutes before bedtime. As long as I am consistent with these "dailies" then I don't get behind or "chopped up." If you have a set routine and goal then it is a lot harder to get sidetracked. WHEN I get sidetracked by the kids' needs, then I have found it a lot easier to get back to what I was doing because I have a set routine. I break everything down into little tasks. Once I started doing my daily routines for 1 week then my weekly cleaning day only took half a day! Each week it takes less and less time. You should spend no longer than 10 minutes on each task. Done is better than perfect!

Good luck. Training those kids can be very rewarding!!

Dejunking and Maintenance

The best way I found to start was just to pick an area and start. Throw away what you haven't looked at for 2 years. I know some say a year, but I'm sentimental. Pick a closet or a dresser or a counter top—get rid of what you just don't need.

That is easier said than done . . . steel yourself. I can't remember what I threw away four years ago when I started. I guess that means I really didn't need it nor do I miss it. It kind of gets easier as you go.

Please note I said I started four years ago. I still have some sacred cows I can't bring myself to do yet. Right now I am just focusing on upkeep of what I have accomplished. That's enough pressure for me for right now. Once you get an area completely cleaned out, just take a couple of seconds a day to make sure it stays that way. Some areas that are high maintenance (i.e. kitchen, living room, bedroom) take longer naturally.

Get Kids Busy

Consider this your first kick if that's what you want and need. We usually don't kick anyone, just nudge them along. Get those children busy. They need to help. They live there and benefit from what does get done so make them help. Jobs posted for each according to age. Have a family meeting and explain what you are going to try to do in your "HOME" and what you expect from each. Then post their jobs. Some might like doing some things the other wouldn't.

When we were kids we had jobs. But my brother took the inside jobs that were my sister's, because she loved yard work. Still does. Her yard is to die for. He loved baking and cleaning floors and would do anything inside

Mom asked as long as it wasn't yard work. So talk it over and see what you can get them to do and make them do it or pay the price. You decide what that should be. Good luck. And you write down a schedule and make yourself do it.

Take Away Treats

Heather—these two girls of yours . . . I'm sure that, being the caring and conscientious mum that you obviously are (you DON'T need to feel guilty, btw), and simply by cheering every time either one of them takes on some chore, those kids will grow up knowing that it's okay to help out and that doing so will help them feel good about themselves (cheers or moans have a lifelong echo). If they grow up to be slobs (unlikely) it'll be their choice. And, ultimately, you have to let them choose their own lifestyles, or they will either rebel against your control or give up the struggle and seek co-dependent relationships all their lives! BUT they are kids, and they are living in your house and if their mess intrudes on your space YOU CAN SAY SO!! (Without guilt!) Why should they dictate the look of your home? Don't you deserve their respect? (Rhetorical question—OF COURSE you do!!!!!!!!)

I recommend bribery and corruption for any kid who doesn't feel like pulling their weight in the house! There's an old Russian saying: He who does not work, does not eat! I'm not suggesting you starve your kids until they tidy their rooms or scrub the footprints off the carpet! But you could try depriving them of treats (pizza, sweets, chocolate, cinema, outings) or privileges (television, friends over, later nights) in return for unhelpfulness, rudeness or intense slobdom.

Good luck!

Cleanup "Game"

I just forwarded a post to a friend of mine who needs to clean her house. She has 3 girls who contribute to the mess. It's about crisis cleaning and using 15 minute intervals to do different jobs. I have come up with an idea to help her out. Her girls like to come to my house and haven't been here in months. She and I have decided to make the cleaning process a game and the grand prize will be a barbecue at my house. Each person will get a different area to work on each 15 minutes and we will all take our breaks together. I am bringing music and told her to decide on some snack rewards for the breaks. I plan on starting off with each of them discarding 27 things and then on to the 15 minute cleaning. I told her to tell the girls it is a game and what the grand prize is. She is making up a list of all that needs to be done. I figure if each girl is doing something different for only 15 minutes they won't get bored and won't get in each other's way. We are both very excited about this venture.

The day started off slow. My friend was supposed to call me at 9 A.M. to wake me. They had a power outage and she overslept and called me at 10. I got up but wasn't feeling good so I took longer to get ready. I left here a little after 1 for the 45–60 minute trip. Got to the bridge and got stuck in traffic. Then once I was on my way there was more traffic—graduation day. I got there around 3 but had called earlier and told them to do a 27 fling boogie each. They made snacks which were supposed to be for break time but the youngest was eating them anyway. She is the best worker so it was okay. Walked in and it was as I had expected—maybe worse. Started to take some before pictures but my batteries were dead. The spare set I kept didn't last much longer so I didn't get all the pictures I wanted. We did get some new ones later in the day and I got some before and after pictures.

So we started. I assigned each person a different job/room. I ended up just letting them do what they wanted in each area and every 15 minutes they switched rooms. The 4th 15 minutes was break time. The girls were not as thrilled about doing this but they all listened to me and did work. One girl worked slower and I needed to check on her if she wasn't in sight. I even got the husband to clean cat litter boxes. Things were going right along and then the mom said one of the cats got loose. The girls ran out and got the cat.

We went out for dinner, came back and finished up some of the cleaning and I took pictures. We got both bathrooms cleaned, both hallways better than they were and the living room and dining area was much neater. We might have gotten more done if the cat hadn't gotten loose. There is also much to do. Not that I am a cleanie but I can advise how they can get/keep things nice. I told them that they needed to do some daily cleaning chores and that they all should participate. Since there are 5 of them we picked 10 areas/chores that needed to be done each day just to maintain. Since the litter boxes are the least favorite I decided that no one person should be assigned that everyday (I have to do it but I have no one else to help). The youngest child came up with writing the chores on popsicle sticks. Each person will pick 2 sticks each day and those will be the chores they need to do. This way it's the luck of the draw and no one can say I always have to do this chore. They do what they pick.

This morning I got a cheery call from my friend making sure I got home okay. (I was there until 2:30 A.M.) She also told me that they were still cleaning.

When the Little Critters Are Capable of Doing Certain Jobs

A mom writes about her teens:

I have found that I get most co-operation from them if I make their tasks small and manageable with a definite end in sight. For instance if they are looking forward to a particular activity, I might say WHEN you have brought down all the laundry, THEN we will watch TV, eat dinner, whatever. Most tasks can be broken down to take ten minutes or less, and this keeps them motivated because they see a beginning and an end.

I make sure that they can see that the task can be completed soon, and that they will be rewarded WHEN it is completed. If it is seen to be an open ended job, then they are far less likely to work quickly and efficiently as they can see no end in sight. Also if I remove privileges, then I end up with a sulky child, and more often than not I forget what he is not supposed to be allowed to do, so then I get angry at myself and find I am putting myself under more pressure.

Age-Appropriate Jobs

At age 2 or 3 (some can be done at a younger age)

Carry things for you
Pick up toys
Get out and put away diapers
Put soiled clothes in the dirty-clothes hamper
Help unload the dishwasher
Help set the table
Feed and water pets
Run errands such as getting things and putting things away for parents
Help put groceries away
Play at sweeping and gardening, using small broom and shovel
Pull up bed clothes
Get out and put away shoes

At ages 4 to 6 children can continue all of the above tasks and add the following. The child will need training and supervision until you are sure he or she is capable. Have things set up so the child has age-appropriate equipment and can reach what he or she needs to do the work.

    Wipe tables and counters
    Help make beds
    Put away clothes
    Carry things to and from car
    Take clothes out of the dryer
    Clear some dishes from table after a meal
    Fold towels and wash clothes
    Help in simple cooking skills
    Water plants
    Put clothes in proper light or dark clothes hamper
    Help with vacuuming, sweeping, and dusting
    Help with younger children in the family
    Work with you in gardening and yard work
    Wash the floor with help
    Put dishes in dishwasher
    Help wash and dry dishes by hand
    Measure soap and start dishwasher
    Empty dishwasher and stack dishes on the counter
    Hang up towel and washcloth after bath
    Fix self simple lunch

At ages 7 to 10 children can continue all the above tasks and add the following.

    Keep room neat
    Put clean laundry away
    Help wash and vacuum car
    Wash dishes
    Read and follow simple recipes

Do simple meal preparation tasks
Run washer and dryer
Help change sheets on bed
Help with projects around the house
Establish personal hygiene habits (bathing, brushing teeth, hair, etc.)

At ages 11 to 15 children can do all of the above plus:

Clean bathrooms once a week
Clean closet and drawers (often with help)
Baby-sit
Plan menu
Buy groceries for menu
Cook simple meals
Begin baking
Wash and wax the car
Mow lawn

At ages 16 to 18 young people can do the work of adults. A well-trained sixteen year old should be able to manage the whole house in the place of an adult. If one parent should have to be away, say on a trip or in the hospital, the older teen could and should be capable of handling what needs to be done so that when the parent returns, neither the family nor the house will have suffered. (The teen may be somewhat the worse for the wear but wiser.)

Run errands (by car when old enough to drive alone)
Manage cash flow, banking, and money in general
Shop for groceries and clothes
Maintain the car

Be able to manage the house, car, and yard by delegation when necessary

Offer good advice in family discussions and problem solving

Organize to move to college

Books That Can Really Help

The books listed here are a sampling of the variety of books available for many ages, many topics (both problems and positive developmental), and many philosophical approaches. There is much help available to keep us on a good path as we raise our children.

Other Books by Sandra

Messie No More. Grand Rapids: Revell, 1989.
> A book that looks at the whys of the "Messie Mindset" and shows how to set yourself free.

Messies Motivator. Grand Rapids: Revell, 1996.
> Designed to motivate those who have started cleaning and then dropped into a more unproductive way of life.

The New Messies Manual: The Procrastinator's Guide to Good Housekeeping. 3rd ed. Grand Rapids: Revell, 2000.

When You Live with a Messie. Grand Rapids: Revell, 1984.

Helps people who have a messie spouse.

Organizing

Mendelson, Cheryl. *Home Comforts—The Art and Science of Keeping House.* New York: Scribner, 1999.

An encyclopedia covering more details than you will ever wish to know. However, having the official word on all aspects of housekeeping does give a sense of confidence whether you use many of them or not.

Morgenstern, Julie. *Organizing from the Inside Out.* New York: Henry Holt and Co., 1998.

Schofield, Deniece. *Confessions of a Happily Organized Family.* Cincinnati: Writer's Digest, 1984.

Sprinkle, Patricia H. *Women Who Do Too Much.* Grand Rapids: Zondervan, 1992.

A book for women who want to evaluate many areas of their lives with the idea of restoring sanity and balance.

Discipline

Coloroso, Barbara. *Kids Are Worth It, Giving Your Child the Gift of Inner Discipline.* San Francisco: Avon, 1995.

Forehand, Rex L. *Parenting the Strong-Willed Child: The Clinically Proven Five-Week Program for Parents of Two-to-Six-Year-Olds.* San Francisco: McGraw Hill, 1996.

Leman, Dr. Kevin. *Making Children Mind without Losing Yours*. Grand Rapids: Revell, 1984.

Taffel, Dr. Ron. *The Second Family: How Adolescent Power Is Challenging the American Family*. New York: St. Martin's Press, 2001.

A heartwarming and enlightening book. The author roots for both the parent and the teen. Written wisely and compassionately about how the parents can bond with teens, can "know" them with and through their teens' friends.

Wychoff, Jerry, et al. *Discipline Without Shouting or Spanking: Practical Solutions to the Most Common Preschool Behavior Problems*. New York: Simon & Schuster, 1985.

Special Needs in Discipline

The following are books for dealing with difficult children. When everything you have tried has failed, look into these for guidance. Parents dealing with this issue are fortunate to have so much help available with approaches that should meet varying needs of both parents and children.

Bodenhamer, Gregory. *Parent in Control*. New York: Fireside, 1995.

A book for restoring order in your home and creating a loving relationship with preteens and teens who are out of control. It may help when nothing else has. Only for really difficult cases.

Clark, Lynn. *SOS! Help for Parents*. 2nd ed. Bowling Green, Ky.: Parents Press, 1996.

This book deals with specific parenting problems as well as the difficult and strong-willed child.

Dobson, James C. *Parenting Isn't for Cowards*. Dallas: Word Publishing, 1987.

An interesting, helpful, and informative book which investigates how to deal with strong-willed children, a longtime subject of study by Dr. Dobson, founder and president of Focus on the Family.

———. *Solid Answers*. Wheaton, Ill.: Tyndale, 1997.

Dr. Dobson answers tough questions facing today's families from a Christian perspective. Includes a chapter on attention deficit disorder in children and a lot of information about discipline. Covers younger children and teens.

Freed, Jeffrey and Laurie Parsons. *Right-Brained Children in a Left-Brained World*. New York: Simon & Schuster, 1997.

This book helps parents to unlock the potential of an ADD child.

Phelan, Thomas W. *1-2-3 Magic: Effective Discipline for Children 2–12*. Glen Ellyn, Ill.: Child Management Inc., 1995.

How to get your children to stop doing what you don't want and start doing what you do want them to do.

Turecki, Stanley and Leslie Tonner. *The Difficult Child*. rev. ed. New York: Bantam, 1989.

This will help parents understand and manage hard to raise children.

Techniques for Chores

Lott, Lynn and Riki Intner. *Chores without Wars*. Rocklin, Calif.: Prima, 1997.

This book takes a positive approach to turning reluctant dads and kids into enthusiastic team players. Excellent approach to family cooperation using communication and plans that work to everybody's benefit.

Sprinkle, Patricia H. *Children Who Do Too Little*. Grand Rapids: Zondervan, 1996.

In this book, Sprinkle shows why and how parents should teach their children household skills. A practical book with helpful hints.

Building Character

Barnes, Dr. Bob. *Ready for Responsibility*. Grand Rapids: Zondervan, 1997.

This is an excellent resource for parents who want their children to grow up ready for marriage and adult responsibilities.

Cloud, Henry and John Townsend. *Boundaries with Kids*. Grand Rapids: Zondervan, 1998.

Establish healthy boundaries with your kids that will help develop a positive relationship between you and your child.

———. *Raising Great Kids*. Grand Rapids: Zondervan, 1999.

Faber, Adele and Elaine Mazlish. *How to Talk So Kids Will Listen & Listen So Kids Will Talk*. San Francisco: Avon, 1999.

This is specifically for parents of preteens and teens.

Fortune, Don and Katie Fortune. *Discovering Your Children's Gifts*. Grand Rapids: Chosen Books, 1989.

This is a thirteen-week study guide to help parents discover and develop the gifts given to them by God.

Whiting, Karen. *Family Devotional Builder*. Peabody, Mass.: Hendrickson, 2000.

This is an organized year of creative, easy to do, family devotions for families with elementary-aged children.

Great Web Sites That Can Really Help

http://www.messies.com
http://www.amazon.com/parenting-and-families
http://www.shesintouch.com
http://www.clutterless.org
http://www.organizedhome.com
http://www.ParentingQA.com
http://www.mommytips.com
http://www.organizetips.com
http://www.choresandrewards.com
http://www.myparentime.com
http://www.momtomom.com
http://www.backincontrol.com
http://www.family.go.com

You'll find more great books, articles, excerpts, and interviews in Amazon.com's Parenting & Families section.

Chore Charts

There are many ways to keep track of chores for families.

- A bag with chores in it. Each person takes two and does them. This works best if all the people doing chores possess about the same ability level. Then it will not matter which chores they get.
- Placing cards on ring. Make one ring of cards for each child. Have one card for each day. If the child finishes the chores for that day, put a sticker on the back. If they don't, no sticker. This will help you to see if there are days when it is harder for one child to get his chores done. Another way to use this is to put one chore on each card and place a sticker or mark on the back each time the chore is done. This will help you see if there is one specific chore a child is having difficulty completing.
- Put snapshots of what the completed chore should look like on cards. This will help visually oriented children as well as those who cannot read. Using this, they have a goal to create something based on

the picture they see. A picture of a set table will show the child which side of the plate each piece of silverware goes and exactly what is expected.

- Use a picture chore chart like the rainbow on page 231. The child colors each part of the picture as they complete chores. Chores done only once or twice a week could be put on the clouds or the sun.

- On a race-car chart on page 232 the child completes the race by coloring each square as the chore is completed. This chore chart lends itself easily to rewarding the child for completing his chores as quickly as possible.

- The charts on page 233 can be used in a couple of ways. One chart can be made for each person and daily chores can be filled down the chart. As the chore is finished the block for that day is either checked or marked with a sticker on the block. The second way to use the chart is to list chores down the chart and fill in a family member's name for each day. As each person completes his chore he covers his name with a sticker.

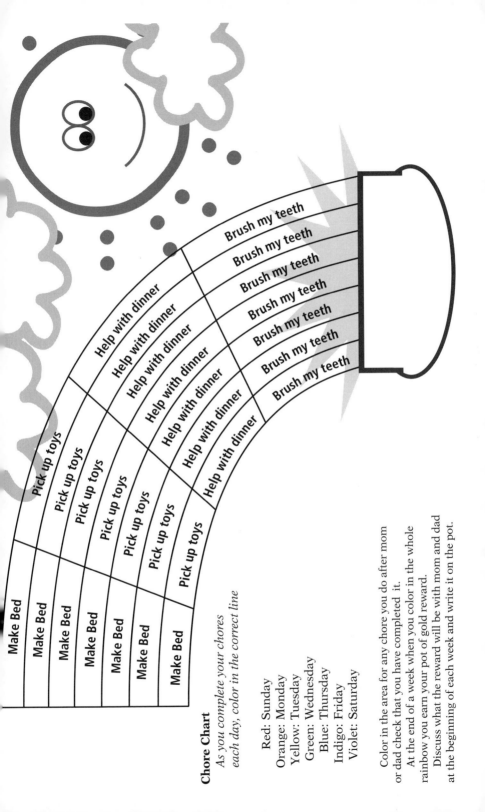

Chore Chart

*As you complete your chores
each day, color in the correct line*

Red: Sunday
Orange: Monday
Yellow: Tuesday
Green: Wednesday
Blue: Thursday
Indigo: Friday
Violet: Saturday

Color in the area for any chore you do after mom
or dad check that you have completed it.

At the end of a week when you color in the whole
rainbow you earn your pot of gold reward.

Discuss what the reward will be with mom and dad
at the beginning of each week and write it on the pot.

(Chart rows, each day:)

Make Bed — Pick up toys — Help with dinner — Brush my teeth

Start your engines and get those chores done. As you complete each chore move your race car further by coloring in the next block.

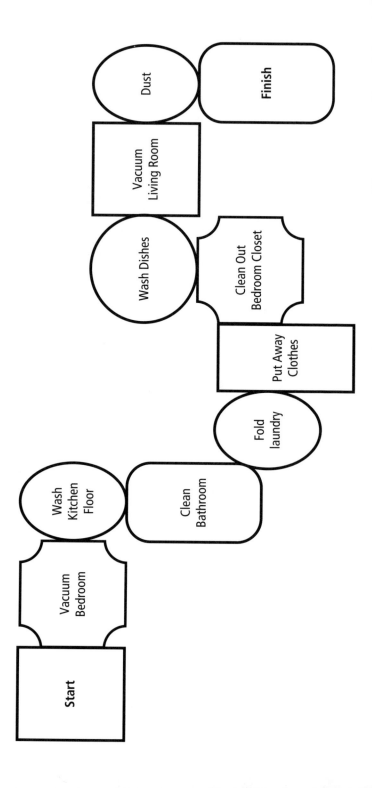

Start

Vacuum Bedroom

Wash Kitchen Floor

Clean Bathroom

Fold laundry

Put Away Clothes

Clean Out Bedroom Closet

Wash Dishes

Vacuum Living Room

Dust

Finish

Personal Chart

	Sunday	Monday	Tuesday	Wednesday	Thursday	Friday	Saturday
Wash dishes							
Make bed							
Pick up toys							
Put away clothes							

Family Chart

	Sunday	Monday	Tuesday	Wednesday	Thursday	Friday	Saturday
Help with dinner	Bobby	Suzy	Peter	Bobby	Dad	Suzy	Peter
Fold laundry	Mom		Bobby	Suzy	Peter	Dad	
Load dishwasher	Suzy	Peter	Bobby	Dad	Mom	Bobby	Suzy
Trash		Bobby			Peter		
Unload dishwasher	Peter	Bobby	Suzy	Peter	Dad	Suzy	
Wash table	Bobby	Suzy	Peter	Bobby	Suzy	Peter	Dad
Set table	Suzy	Peter	Dad	Suzy	Bobby	Bobby	Peter
Clean bathroom			Suzy			Suzy	
Vacuum		Mom		Peter		Bobby	

Family Contract

Purpose: _____

What is the higher reason the child should do the job? To please mom/to take care of my friend (pet) as I should/to prepare for adult life/to act as a team member/etc.

Job to be done: _____
    Place: _____
    Completion time limit: _____
        Prompt timing is important for some jobs.
    Duration of contract: _____
        Limit the duration to week, month, etc.

Clarification of job: _____
_____
_____

    Make the job details very clear so there is no misunderstanding.

Personal benefit: _____
    How good it will make the child feel.

Reward for keeping the contract: _____

Consequence for not keeping the contract: _____

About the Author

Organizing expert Sandra Felton is the author of several books, including *Messie No More, The Messies Motivator, When You Live with a Messie,* and *The New Messies Manual.* She is the founder of Messies Anonymous, which helps others who struggle with disorganization to get and stay organized.

A graduate of Columbia International University with a graduate degree from the University of Miami, Sandra is a career high school teacher. She is the mother of three adult children and lives with her husband in Miami. Recently she left teaching to speak, write, and give full time to helping others get organized.

About Messies Anonymous

The purpose of Messies Anonymous is to help people move from a lifestyle of out-of-control clutter to a life of productive and satisfying order. Among the ways that people find help are twelve-step self-help groups, the MA ClutterBuddy program, a quarterly newsletter, and an interactive web site (www.messies.com).

Some books written by Sandra Felton that are available through Messies Anonymous are:

Time Management for the Harried Teacher
Hope for the Hopeless Messie

Stop Messing Around and Organize to Write

Why Can't I Get Organized? (for **ADD** readers)

The Whiz Bang Guide on How to Organize Time and Things

Audio and video tapes by Sandra Felton are also available. For a free introductory newsletter and other information about Messies Anonymous, write MA, 5025 SW 114 Ave., Miami, FL 33165 or log on to: www.messies .com.

Speaking

Funny and practical, Sandra enjoys bringing her powerful message of organizational control to business and professional groups, mental health organizations, church women's ministries, and Christian gatherings through speaking. If you would like Sandra to serve as a speaker, you may contact her directly at:

Sandra Felton
5025 SW 114 Ave.
Miami, FL 33165
SRFMA@aol.com
FAX: 305-273-7671